THE PROPHETS

*Their Personalities
and Teachings*

THE
PROPHETS
Their Personalities and Teachings

by BERYL D. COHON

EST. 1854

BLOCH PUBLISHING COMPANY
NEW YORK

PRINTED IN THE UNITED STATES OF AMERICA
BY GANIS AND HARRIS, NEW YORK

TO

SALLY

PREFACE

AT A TIME when booted warriors are trampling under
foot all that civilized men hold sacred and the anchors of
faith are dragging in the storm, the Hebrew prophets
speak a commanding word. They speak of God and conscience, they denounce the vested evils, excoriate the mighty
and the powerful, repudiate the immoral religions, and
plead for justice, mercy and humility as the will of God
in the affairs of men. They stretch far horizons before
those who have eyes to see; they speak of a new heaven
and a new earth to those who have the imagination to per-
ceive. In an age when nations are snarling at each other
across every frontier, when races are at each other's
throats, and classes are in conflict, the nobility of mind
and majesty of speech of the Hebrew prophets breathe
healing and strength.

The present author has sought to delineate the personalities of the prophets against the backgrounds of their
times. Historic summaries are given in bold outline. To
capture the authentic spirit of the prophets he has resorted to generous quotations from Bible text. Thus each
prophet speaks his own message in his own words against
the events of his day.

Most of the present volume has grown out of the author's experience in teaching the prophets to lay classes
and to undergraduates. He has, therefore, avoided the

technical and the academic, and emphasized the moral realities as embodied in their personalities and words.

The Bible text is that of the Jewish Publication Society of America. (Where the verse number of the Biblical passages in this book is not the same as the King James version, the latter is given in parentheses.) The more successful translations made by Bible scholars are utilized, though sparingly.

The author's indebtedness to the masters who have cultivated the field of Bible study and brought forth an abundant harvest will be apparent to all who are acquainted with modern scholarship. Few laymen appreciate the prodigious and consecrated labor of these toilers in the vineyard. They have reclaimed the Bible for the modern mind. To his brother and teacher, Professor Samuel S. Cohon, he is indebted not only for reading most of the manuscript, but for a far larger gift: it is he who first revealed to him the vision of Hebrew prophecy. To his students at Boston University, to the men, women and children of Temple Israel, Boston, who were in his classes, and to the new group of students and friends at Temple Sinai, he is indebted for their healthy skepticism, which required him to seek the human in the divine and to phrase his findings in every-day terms.

B. D. C.

October, 1939.

Boston, Massachusetts.

PREFACE TO THE 1960 REISSUE

The primary aim of this volume is to reveal the vision of the Hebrew prophets—its power and its urgency for our time. The world was in the terror of the Second World War when this book appeared in 1939. Since then the crescendo of moral insanity has rocked our civilization to its foundations, turning our earth into a seething volcano. The dreaded visions of apocalyptic destruction have come true. Millions of men, women and children have been pulverized, gassed in crematoria—systematically, scientifically; cities with all their treasures of life and the achievement of the ages have been blown into ashes; atomic bombs are hanging over our heads, atomic fallout is poisoning the generations yet unborn. The words of the prophet haunt the mind:

Multitudes, multitudes in the valley of decision! For the day of the Lord is near in the valley of decision.

It is the author's prayer that by means of his book a few people, here and there—in a synagogue, a church, in a class, in a discussion group—may be stimulated into reading the Hebrew prophets and catch their vision of the time "when none shall hurt and none destroy in all my holy mountain; for the earth shall be filled with the knowledge of God as the waters cover the sea."

Since 1939, Bible scholars have given us fresh analyses of the literary expressions of Hebrew prophecy. The student who is interested in the technical aspects of the prophetic literature—its history, its forms, its texts—should study these works. Several titles published recently have therefore been added to the original bibliography. Each of these titles gives further bibliographies, or makes reference to more recent works. The present volume, however, is not concerned especially with literary criticism; its primary concern is the moral content of Hebrew prophecy—its tantalizing vision of a new heaven and a new earth, under the sovereignty of the Righteous Judge. The magnificent lines of the prophet Habakkuk may be taken as the text of all the Hebrew prophets, and they ring with peculiar urgency in our day; this is what the author has sought to reveal:

I will stand upon the watch,
And set me upon the tower,
And will look out to see what He will speak by me,
And what I shall answer when I am reproved.
And the Lord answered me and said:
'Write the vision,
And make it plain upon tables,
That a man may read it swiftly.
For the vision is yet of the appointed time,
And it declareth of the end, and doth not lie;
Though it tarry, wait for it;
Because it will surely come, it will not delay.'

BERYL D. COHON

Temple Sinai,
Brookline, Massachusetts
June, 1960

CONTENTS

XI

ABBREVIATIONS

CB   *The Cambridge Bible for Schools and Colleges,* General Editor for Old Testament, A. F. Kirkpatrick. Cambridge: University Press. New York: The Macmillan Company.

HERE Hastings, *Encyclopedia of Religion and Ethics.* Edinburgh: T. & T. Clark. New York: Charles Scribner's Sons.

ICC   *International Critical Commentary.* Edinburgh: T. & T. Clark. New York: Charles Scribner's Sons.

BIBLICAL ABBREVIATIONS

Cant.	Canticles	*Hab.*	Habakkuk	*Nah.*	Nahum
Chron.	Chronicles	*Hag.*	Haggai	*Nehem.*	Nehemiah
Dan.	Daniel	*Hos.*	Hosea	*Num.*	Numbers
Deut.	Deuteronomy	*Isa.*	Isaiah	*Obad.*	Obadiah
Eccl.	Ecclesiastes	*Jer.*	Jeremiah	*Prov.*	Proverbs
Esth.	Esther	*Josh.*	Joshua	*Ps.*	Psalms
Ex.	Exodus	*Judg.*	Judges	*Sam.*	Samuel
Ezek.	Ezekiel	*Lam.*	Lamentations	*Zech.*	Zechariah
Gen.	Genesis	*Lev.*	Leviticus	*Zeph.*	Zephaniah
		Mal.	Malachi		

I

CHARACTERISTICS OF THE PROPHETS

By a prophet the Lord brought Israel out of Egypt,
And by a prophet was he preserved.

Hosea 12:14 (13).

THE Hebrew prophets were uncompromising individual-
ists. In thought, in speech, in conduct every true prophet
obeyed the will of God as he understood it. There was
nothing conventional about the Hebrew literary prophets;
they were not interested in the approval or disapproval of
the world. One force held them enthralled: the word of
God. Nevertheless, certain characteristics distinguish the
whole group.

First, the prophet is carried by a divine compulsion
that gives him no peace, no rest, no respite. He is possessed
by the word of God. "Thus saith the Lord!" is the prophetic refrain. Not the prophet but God is speaking; the
prophet is only the mouthpiece of the Eternal. "Behold,
I have put My words in thy mouth," Jeremiah hears God
say to him.[1] The very word "prophet," in its native Greek,
means one who speaks for or in behalf of another.[2] He is
the proclaimer of a revelation; he is the instrument, at
times the unwilling instrument, in the hands of the Ruler

[1] 1:9.
[2] The Hebrew word for Prophet is *nabi.* See Gesenius, *Hebrew and Chaldee Lexicon to the Old Testament Scriptures* on this word.

1

of men and nations. He speaks because the word of God within him will not permit him to keep silent. "The lion hath roared, who shall not fear? The Lord God hath spoken, who shall not prophesy?"[3] The prophet is in the grip of a supreme power. "The Lord spoke thus to me while the hand grasped me," says Isaiah.[4] In season and out of season he must speak. The destinies of men and nations hang on the words God has put into his mouth. "Thou hast seized me, O Lord, and hast enthralled me; Thou hast laid Thine hand upon me and hast overpowered me,"[5] moaned Jeremiah in a moment of soul-searching. He could not be silent and play safe:

> If I say: "I will not make mention of Him,
> Nor speak any more in His name,"
> Then there is in my heart as it were a burning fire
> Shut up in my bones,
> And I weary myself to hold it in,
> But cannot.[6]

Second, the prophet is a critic of the social order. He does not deal with abstractions; metaphysical terms are entirely missing from his vocabulary. He does not discuss theologies as such; he does not plead for principles in the abstract. Always his message is aimed at the specific evils in the life about him. He arises in days of national crisis and speaks his mind—or, better, the mind of God—upon particular events. He denounces kings to their faces for specific acts, rebukes bluntly the mighty of the earth, and harangues the mobs for their idolatries.

[3] Amos 3:8. [4] 8:11.
[5] 20:7. (*See* Moses Buttenwieser, *The Prophets of Israel,* p. 9 for translation).
[6] 20:9.

One or two familiar scenes from the Bible will show the mettle of the prophet. Bathsheba was the wife of Uriah the Hittite, who was doggedly faithful to his king, David. The monarch was enamoured of Bathsheba, who, it would seem, did not resist his advances. When she informed him that she was with child by him, David flattered her husband with special attention and promoted him to an especially dangerous position in a war then in progress. Uriah fell in battle and David inherited his wife. Then "the Lord sent Nathan unto David. And he came unto him, and said unto him:

There were two men in one city: the one rich, and the other poor. The rich man had exceeding many flocks and herds; but the poor man had nothing, save one little ewe lamb, which he had bought and reared; and it grew up together with him, and with his children; it did eat of his own morsel, and drank of his own cup, and lay in his bosom, and was unto him as a daughter. And there came a traveller unto the rich man, and he spared to take of his own flock and of his own herd, to dress for the wayfaring man that was come unto him, but took the poor man's lamb, and dressed it for the man that was come to him. And David's anger was greatly kindled against the man; and he said to Nathan: "As the Lord liveth, the man that hath done this deserveth to die; and he shall restore the lamb four fold, because he did this thing, and because he had no pity."

And Nathan said to David: "Thou art the man!"[7]

Naboth had a vineyard which adjoined the king's palace. King Ahab wanted this vineyard; he offered Naboth a fair price for it, but Naboth refused. It was his ancestral

[7] II Sam. 12:1–8.

estate and he could not part with it. Jezebel, who had a
great deal of initiative and no conscience, came to her husband's assistance. She set a trap for Naboth. Forging
her husband's signature, she arranged for a state function,
invited high society, placed Naboth in a conspicuous position, and surrounded him with men hired to testify
against him. In the course of the evening, they raised a
tumult and charged Naboth with treason. Naboth was
stoned and Ahab inherited his vineyard. Then "the word
of the Lord came to Elijah the Tishbite, saying:

Arise, go down to meet Ahab, king of Israel, who
dwelleth in Samaria; behold, he is in the vineyard of Naboth, whither he is gone down to take possession of it.
And thou shalt speak unto him, saying: "Thus saith the
Lord: Hast thou killed, and also taken possession?" and
thou shalt speak unto him, saying: "Thus saith the Lord:
In the place where dogs licked the blood of Naboth shall
dogs lick thy blood, even thine." And Ahab said to Elijah:
"Hast thou found me, O mine enemy?" And he answered:
"I have found thee; because thou hast given thyself over
to do that which is evil in the sight of the Lord."[8]

Wherever wrong appeared, there the prophet raised his
voice in divine protest. The point must not be overlooked
that as critic of the social order the prophet was tempered
by the will of God as he understood it. He was not a secu-
lar critic of the established society, not merely a disgruntled
individual who was against things, not a critic guided by
a political or economic philosophy of his own. He was
guided by the will of God. He applied the plumbline of
the divine will to all things and found the entire social

[8]I Kings 21:17-21.

structure crooked. If he was a critic of the existing civilization, it was because the word of God burned within him, and when he spoke as a social reformer, he prefaced his words with divine authority: "Thus saith the Lord." He was never out of touch with events, and he was never out of touch with the will of God.

Third, the prophet often predicted the future. On this point a word of caution must be spoken promptly. The literary prophet was not a fortune-teller. He did not predict the future by some occult power. But he did envisage the future, and he announced his vision as an accomplished fact. Amos chanted a dirge over fallen Israel while the nation was at the height of her worldly power. "In those days" and "It shall come to pass at the end of days" are characteristic expressions in the prophetic literature. However, they foretold not isolated events but the realization of the will of God. The prophet saw all things from the standpoint of divine will. Every aspect of the life of man and nations, even of nature, was controlled by moral cause and effect. By understanding the causes, one might envisage the effects. The fates of nations were determined by a sort of moral determinism. Convinced of that, the prophet could and did foretell the future.

It is a significant fact to note that as *foretellers* the prophets were failures. Their predictions went wild again and again. Jeremiah especially seemed to have been inept at the art. Prediction was not their special gift nor interest. Their chief concern was to bring the present into line with the will of God. "The prophets were not gifted in the art of reading the details of the future to any greater extent than experts along these lines elsewhere in the world," writes a distinguished scholar.[9] "In so far as they did indicate the general direction of human progress, it was due to the fact that they were better qualified students of the present than others. They were in profounder sympathy with the eternal purpose, and by keen discernment of its workings in the past and present were able to forecast the main lines of operation in the immediate future."

Moreover, the future is only the present in the making. By painting the days to come, the prophet gave warning of the course of events of his day. His predictions were therefore means of enforcing his message. And his predictions were largely conditional—his message heeded, the announced evil might be averted. Jeremiah states it clearly. Speaking in the name of God, he says: "At one instant I may speak concerning a nation, and concerning a kingdom, to pluck up and to break down and to destroy it; but if that nation turn from their evil, because of which I have spoken against it, I repent of the evil that I thought to do unto it. And at one instant I may speak concerning a nation, and concerning a kingdom, to build and to plant it; but if it do evil in My sight, that it hearken not to My voice, then I repent of the good, wherewith I said I would benefit it."[10]

Fourth, the prophets were lonely, solitary men of God. They did not go about in groups; theirs was not a profession that gave a man a colleague. Other prophets of a different mold, of whom we shall speak subsequently, went about in groups; but not the true prophets. They com-

[9] J. M. Powis Smith, *The Prophet and his Problems*, pp. 103-104.
[10] 18:7-11.

muned with God in the silence of the night; haunted by a vision, they were men set apart from their fellows; they were in the busy places of the world—in the market places, at the city gates, in the Temple, even in the palace—but always they were lonely individuals. We know little of their family life. All we have are a few bare facts. But we do know that Amos was a solitary figure, tending his sheep and caring for his sycamores in a land that is described in the Bible as "a waste and howling wilderness." Hosea's family life was tragic. Isaiah, though associating with royalty, kept his own counsel, and could not look at his own children without seeing black doom about to crack over the nation. Jeremiah never married. Why should he bring children into a morally-collapsing world? His own family seems to have persecuted him. "Everyone mocketh me," he complains. Ezekiel must have been surrounded by many people, for he seems to have been the teacher and guide of a people walking in darkness. God himself seemed to have deserted them. Their homes plundered, their state and the Temple of their God in ashes, far from their native haunts, they could not sing the Lord's song in a foreign land. Ezekiel must have shared their sorrow. Of that enchanting singer, commonly called "the second Isaiah," we know nothing at all, not even his name. They were solitary lonely figures—"alone with Thee, my God."[11]

The prophets were men who spoke for God, or in behalf of God; they were the bearers and the preachers of God's word. They came in time of crisis; their words were ad-

---

[11] G. C. Joyce, "Old Testament Prophecy," in Peake, *Commentary on the Bible,* p. 26.

dressed to specific events. These events were either physical or political. An earthquake, a drought, a pestilence, the rise of some political leader who upset the existing order were sure manifestations of the will of God.[12]

[12]*See* George Adam Smith, *The Book of the Twelve Prophets,* Chap. II.

II

MAD ENTHUSIASTS

And Elisha said . . . "bring me a minstrel."
And it came to pass, when the minstrel played,
that the hand of the Lord came upon him.

II KINGS 3:15.

THE literary prophets must not be confused with the professional soothsayers. These were essentially mad enthusiasts who roamed the country in groups and engaged in prediction for a fee. Emotional excitement bordering on insanity characterized their performances. They are branded in the Bible as "false prophets" or "prophets of Baal."

A vivid scene revealing the character of these false prophets and the methods they employed is given in the book of Samuel. Saul, the peasant boy who had been searching for his father's lost asses, was returning home with a crown on his head. The aged Samuel had anointed him first king of Israel. The crown wore heavily upon him. The boy was probably bewildered and fearful. Samuel—judge, priest, prophet, politician—was sending him off with his blessing:

Then Samuel took the vial of oil, and poured it upon his head, and kissed him, and said: "Is it not that the Lord hath anointed thee to be prince over His inheritance? When thou art departed from me today, then thou shalt find two men by the tomb of Rachel, in the border of Ben-

9

jamin at Zelzah; and they will say unto thee: The asses which thou wentest to seek are found; and, lo, thy father hath left off caring for the asses, and is anxious concerning you, saying: What shall I do for my son? Then shalt thou go on forward from thence, and thou shalt come to the terebinth of Tabor, and there shall meet thee there three men going up to God to Beth-el, one carrying three kids, and another carrying three loaves of bread, and another carrying a bottle of wine. And they will salute thee, and give thee two cakes of bread; which thou shalt receive of their hand. After that thou shalt come to the hill of God, where is the garrison of the Philistines; and it shall come to pass, when thou art come thither to the city, that thou shalt meet a band of prophets coming down from the high place with a psaltery, and a timbrel, and a pipe, and a harp, before them; and they will be prophesying. And the spirit of the Lord will come mightily upon thee, and thou shalt prophesy with them, and shalt be turned into another man. And let it be, when these signs are come unto thee, that thou do as thy hand shall find; for God is with thee. And thou shalt go down before me to Gilgal; and, behold, I will come down unto thee, to offer burnt-offerings, and to sacrifice sacrifices of peace-offerings; seven days shalt thou tarry, till I come unto thee, and tell thee what thou shalt do."

And it was so, that when he had turned his back to go from Samuel, God gave him another heart; and all those signs came to pass that day. And when they came thither to the hill, behold, a band of prophets met him; and the spirit of God came mightily upon him, and he prophesied among them. And it came to pass, when all that knew him beforetime saw that, behold, he prophesied with the prophets, then the people said one to another: "What is this that is come unto the son of Kish? Is Saul also among the prophets?"[1]

[1] I Sam. 10:1–12.

Another close view of the "false prophets" and the striking contrast between these professional soothsayers and the "true prophets" is given in the book of Kings. The kings of Judah and Israel had formed an alliance to launch a war of aggression. First, however, they would consult the oracle:

And Jehoshaphat said unto the king of Israel: "Inquire, I pray thee, at the word of the Lord today." Then the king of Israel gathered the prophets together, about four hundred men, and said unto them: "Shall I go against Ramoth-gilead to battle, or shall I forbear?" And they said: "Go up; for the Lord will deliver it into the hand of the king." But Jehoshaphat said: "Is there not here besides a prophet of the Lord, that we might inquire of him?" And the king of Israel said unto Jehoshaphat: "There is yet one man by whom we may inquire of the Lord, Micaiah the son of Imlah; but I hate him; for he doth not prophesy good concerning me, but evil." And Jehoshaphat said: "Let not the king say so." Then the king of Israel called an officer, and said: "Fetch quickly Micaiah the son of Imlah." Now the king of Israel and Jehoshaphat the king of Judah sat each on his throne, arrayed in their robes, in a threshing floor, at the entrance of the gate of Samaria; and all the prophets prophesied before them. And Zedekiah the son of Chenaanah made him horns of iron, and said: "Thus saith the Lord: With these shalt thou gore the Arameans, until they be consumed." And all the prophets prophesied so, saying: "Go up to Ramoth-gilead, and prosper; for the Lord will deliver it into the hand of the king."

And the messenger that went to call Micaiah spoke unto him, saying: "Behold now the words of the prophets declare good unto the king with one mouth, let thy word, I pray thee, be like the word of one of them, and speak thou good." And Micaiah said: "As the Lord liveth, what the Lord saith unto me, that will I speak."[2]

Dressed in wild costume (one of their tribe in the Micaiah story just quoted "made him horns of iron")—they would dance around the altar, shriek and howl in frenzied exaltation, draw blood and rave the word of God.[3]

The contagion of this mob frenzy is humorously reported in the book of I Samuel. The deranged Saul was leading an expedition against young David. Word reached him that David was with Samuel at Naioth in Ramah:

And Saul sent messengers to take David; and when they saw the company of the prophets prophesying, and Samuel standing as head over them, the spirit of God came upon the messengers of Saul, and they also prophesied. And when it was told Saul, he sent other messengers and they also prophesied. And Saul sent messengers again the third time, and they also prophesied.

Then went he also to Ramah, and came to the great cistern, that is in Secu; and he asked and said: "Where are Samuel and David?" And one said: "Behold, they are at Naioth in Ramah." And he went thither to Naioth in Ramah; and the spirit of God came upon him also, and he went on, and prophesied, until he came to Naioth in Ramah. And he also stripped off his clothes, and he also prophesied before Samuel, and lay down naked all that day and all that night. Wherefore they say: "Is Saul also among the prophets?"[4]

The characteristics of the "false prophets" are clearly revealed in these passages and in the several more that

[2] I Kings 22:5-14.
[3] See I Kings 18 for the experience of Elijah with the "prophets of Baal" and note the conduct of these dervishes.
[4] I Sam. 19:20-24.

might be cited. *First,* these soothsayers came in groups. The Bible speaks of "bands of prophets." The Hebrew *hebel n'biim* may be translated as "gangs" or "troupes" or "companies" of prophets. The true prophet stood alone. *Second,* they were professional prophets. They earned their living by prophesying; they were under the constant temptation, therefore, to echo sentiments that would win them larger fees and wider popularity. "Thus saith the king," rather than "Thus saith the Lord" was their inspiration and authority. Micaiah ben Imlah calls them "inspired liars." As for himself, he says, only "What the Lord saith unto me, that will I speak."[5] The nature of genuine prophecy is to be interbound with one's very life. *Third,* the inspiration of the false prophets was usually produced artificially. In the story of Saul, which we have cited, the false prophets are equipped with musical instruments and the purpose of these was to stimulate prophecy. Elisha, asked to prophesy, found himself incapable of it for the reason that he was completely composed, mentally cool and normal in every way. To engage in prophecy one had to be hysterical. "Bring me a minstrel," he says. "And it came to pass, when the minstrel played, that the hand of the Lord came upon him."[6] "An examination of the writings of the great prophets for phenomena of this sort warrants the statement that the greater the prophet was the less recourse did he have to such extraneous support for his message."[7] *Fourth,* the false prophet was in a state of frenzy when speaking his oracle. Samuel tells Saul that when the spirit of prophecy

[5] I Kings 22:14. [6] II Kings 3:15.
[7] J. M. Powis Smith, *The Prophet and his Problems,* p. 47.

shall come over him he will be "turned into another man." As long as one was in the complete control of his mental powers, he could not engage in prophecy of the type exemplified by these enthusiasts. "The characteristic of the true prophet is that he retains his consciousness and self-control under revelation."[8]

This, however, should not be pressed too far. Much of the book of Ezekiel and the inaugural visions of Isaiah and Jeremiah cannot be fully explained unless we recognize the part ecstasy and trance played in the lives of the prophets.

[8]Robertson Smith as quoted by M. Buttenwieser in *The Prophets of Israel,* p. 138. Note also Plato's view of prophecy quoted by Buttenwieser.

III

IDOLATRY

---

*How long halt ye between two opinions? If the Lord be God,
follow Him; but if Baal, follow him. . . . Elijah mocked them
and said: "Cry aloud; for he is a god; either he is musing, or he
is gone aside, or he is on a journey, or peradventure he sleepeth,
and must be awaked."*

I KINGS 18:21, 27.

WE MUST sketch the religious backgrounds to the teachings of the Hebrew literary prophets and note the nature
of the beliefs, practices, and institutions against which
they lashed out with so much passion. Unless we do, we
shall not appreciate the full grandeur of their words. We
must therefore recall the gods and goddesses, the wayside altars and secluded groves that infested Israel and
Judah.

In the year 621 B.C. a religious revolution swept Israel.
It is known as the Reformation of Josiah. It transformed
radically the religious life of the country and affected
—quite violently—the economic structure. Behind this
reformation was the driving power of the prophetic spirit.
We shall discuss it in a later chapter. Here we note the
idolatry it reveals.

The immediate cause for the revolution was the dis-
covery of a document in the Temple at Jerusalem.[1] Work-

[1] II Kings 22:1-23:25. The "Book of the Law" has been identified as
the book of Deuteronomy. For a discussion of this, see S. R. Driver,
Deuteronomy, in *ICC,* Introduction, section 4.

men repairing the Temple came on "a book of the Law," which, it is likely, was planted. It made a sensational impression on the king. A national convention was summoned, and sweeping religious reforms were instituted. The Temple was cleared of its idols. By observing this housecleaning we may gain a measure of insight into the religious practices of the time, against which the prophets stormed.

And the king commanded Hilkiah the high priest and the priests of the second order, and the keepers of the door, to bring forth out of the temple of the Lord all the vessels that were made for Baal, and for the Asherah, and for all the host of heaven; and he burned them without Jerusalem in the fields of Kidron, and carried the ashes of them unto Beth-el. And he put down the idolatrous priests, whom the kings of Judah had ordained to offer in the high places in the cities of Judah, and in the places round about Jerusalem; them also that offered unto Baal, to the sun, and to the moon, and to the constellations, and to all the host of heaven. And he brought out the Asherah from the house of the Lord, without Jerusalem, unto the brook Kidron, and burned it at the brook Kidron, and stamped it small to powder, and cast the powder thereof upon the graves of the common people. And he broke down the houses of the sodomites, that were in the house of the Lord, where the women wove coverings for the Asherah. . . .

And he defied Topheth, which is in the valley of the sun of Hinnom, that no man might make his son or his daughter to pass through the fire to Molech. . . .

And the high places that were before Jerusalem, which were on the right hand of the mount of corruption, which Solomon the king of Israel had builded for Ashtoreth the detestation of the Zidonians, and for Chemosh the detestation of Moab, and for Milcom the abomination of the children of Ammon, did the king defile. And he broke in pieces the pillars, and cut down the Asherim, and filled their places with the bones of men.[2]

We have here a reasonably inclusive assortment of idols and idolatries. These were part of the heritage upon which the Hebrews came when they settled in Canaan. The Promised Land was settled by many peoples. Each locality, each tribe, each country had its own gods, its own body of local traditions, its own recognized shrines, its own fixed ritual. The Hebrew invaders were gradually invaded by these. They came as nomads and in time were transformed into agriculturists. Their religious ideas and practices were transformed accordingly. This process of fusion was a period of stress and strain. Much of the denunciation of the prophets was against this inexorable and inevitable assimilation. In the assortment of deities we see carted out of the Temple with all their furniture, we note the extent to which the local gods and goddesses had invaded the religion of Israel and transformed it.

With these agricultural gods came a set of moral—or, better, immoral—practices which drew the fire of the prophets. There was ample warrant for their fiery denunciation. "By all indications," writes Adolphe Lods, "as is often the case with agricultural religions, Canaanite religion was of an orgiastic nature: the ritual tended to stir up in the worshippers a wild excitement; maddened by the cries, the dances, the wine, they gave themselves up by turns to unbridled merriment and to bloody practices . . . cutting themselves or offering to the gods whatever

[2]II Kings 23:4–14.

they held most dear. For the same reason ecstatic phenomena and sexual excesses seem to have played a large
part in the religious life of the inhabitants of Palestine."[3]
The same scholar continues: "The depravity of the Canaanites was notorious: witness the vices attributed to the
inhabitants of Sodom and Gomorrah, the reason alleged
for their destruction by the fire of Jahweh.[4] . . . The
very religion of the Canaanites with its bloody ritual, its
female deities, its frequent ceremonial orgies, the halo
of sanctity with which it surrounded prostitution, all
tended to foster license rather than to eradicate it."[5]

Let us summon these deities to present themselves one
by one; and let us note, also, what influences they had
upon the moral life of the Canaanitish folk and their
Hebrew imitators.

First come the *Baalim.* The word *baal* means "master,"
"owner," "possessor." It is not a proper name but a title
of divinity found in all branches of the Semitic race. The
Baalim were the masters of field and forest, mountain and
oasis, well and river. Life and death, good fortune and
bad, reproduction, growth, healing, decay were under
their control. We read in the Bible of a Baal of the palm-
tree, a Baal of Lebanon, a Baalath (note the feminine)
of the well; there is a Baal of the dance, another of healing, another of good luck. There were thus sacred trees,
sacred wells, sacred stones, sacred mountains.[6] A spirit
dwelt in them and rendered them taboo. To break this

---

[3]*Israel: From its Beginning to the Middle of the Eighth Century,* p.
102.
  [4]Gen. 13:13; 18:20–21; 19.   [5]Lods, *ibid.,* p. 148.
  [6]Josh. 2:17; 12:7; 19:8; Judg. 8:33; 20:33; II Sam. 5:20, etc. See
Adolphe Lods, *Israel,* especially pp. 83–143; 401–450.

taboo one had to placate the deity, bribe it with offerings and sacrifices of various kinds. Man needed the water of the well, the fruit of the tree, the produce of the field, the offspring of the herd. But these were controlled by spirits—*baalim*—who must not be offended. Therefore one had to ingratiate himself with the deity. Moreover, the farmer was dependent upon these spirits. He was anxious for the well to remain alive, for the tree to be fruitful, for the field to be fertile. Hence one had to set an example in reproduction to the spirit that possessed these; gifts had to be placed upon the altar. A portion of the harvest, or the first-born of the flock and even of humans, was, therefore, offered as sacrifice. This, of course, is the primitive, animistic stage of religion. The prophets did heroic work in dragging mankind out of these abysmal depths.

Along with "the vessels made for Baal," was removed the *Asherah*. This was an altar, probably in the form of a stump of a tree, or a pillar, devoted to the worship of a goddess known by several names: *Asherah, Ashtoreth, Ashtart, Ishtar, Astarte.*[7] This was the female deity. "It would seem," states Professor Lods,[8] "that all these divine female figures, who were in reality various aspects of the fertility principle, tended to merge into a single great female deity, commonly called Astarte. This name, in turn, became . . . a sort of general name for goddess." She was primarily the goddess of sexual love, maternity and fertility. In Babylonian sources she is described as "she who causes to bear," and is depicted as a woman suckling

[7]See art. "Ashtart (Ashtoreth), Astarte" in *HERE.*
[8]*Ibid.,* p. 132.

a child at her breast. She also did service as a goddess of war.

Worship of this deity led to the horrible institution of holy prostitution. Young women were dedicated to this service with all the sanction and halo of religious observance. "And he broke down the houses of the sodomites," we read in the Bible chapter before us,[9] "that were in the house of the Lord, where the women wove coverings for the Asherah." Amos denounces this institution: "A man and his son go unto the same maid to defile My holy name." "They sacrifice with holy harlots," complains Hosea. Repugnant as the institution is to us today, it was respectable and proper in primitive religion. A Moabitish inscription bears the report that when Mesha, the King of Moab, took Nebo from the Israelites, he slew the men but deported the women to dedicate them to the Ashtar-Chemosh deities.[10] Professor Toy writes: "In old Babylonia, Canaan, Syria, Phœnicia, Asia Minor, Armenia, Greece, and now in West Africa and India, we find officially appointed 'sacred' women, a part of whose religious duty it was or is to offer themselves to men. The service in ancient times was not regarded as degrading; on the contrary, maidens of the noblest families were sometimes so dedicated and the role of devotees might be continued in a family for generations. Such service was sometimes a necessary preliminary to marriage."[11]

The assortment of deities included, also, the gods of the sun, moon, the seven planets, the Zodiac. There must

---

[9]II Kings 23:7. [10]See *CB* to Hosea 4:14.
[11]Crawford Howell Toy, *Introduction to the History of Religions*, p. 516. See paragraphs 1065–1066 and note references to Westermark and Frazer.

have been, further, the more native idolatry of Israel: the sacred calf and the sacred bull. The bull was worshipped especially at Beth-el, the national shrine where Amos made his dramatic appearance.

And they forsook all the commandments of the Lord their God, and made them molten images, even two calves, and made an Asherah, and worshipped all the host of heaven, and served Baal and they caused their sons and their daughters to pass through the fire, and used divination and enchantments, and gave themselves over to do that which was evil in the sight of the Lord, to provoke Him.[12]

The historian goes on to narrate of the further idolatries practised by the Israelites:

He removed the high places, and broke the pillars, and cut down the Asherah; and he broke in pieces the brazen serpent that Moses had made; for unto those days the children of Israel did offer to it; and it was called Nehushtan.[13]

To this horde of gods and goddesses and evil spirits must be added the most horrible of all: Chemosh, "the obscene dread of Moab's sons"; Milcom, "the abomination of the Ammonites"; and Moloch, the Phœnician deity who demanded the first-born males:

> Moloch, horrid king, besmear'd with blood
> Of human sacrifice and parents' tears.[14]

Perhaps the last three were one monstrosity passing under different names. The worship of these required

[12]II Kings 17:16–17.   [13]II Kings 18:4.
[14]Milton, *Paradise Lost*, Book I, Lines 392–3.

human sacrifice. Recent excavations bear mute testimony
to this horror.[15] Many passages in the Bible testify to
child-sacrifice in ancient Israel. We read of back-sliding
kings who made their sons "to pass through fire." Jephthah sacrificed his daughter—his only child—because
he dared not violate his rash oath to his god.[16] This in-
stance is all the more repugnant because the young woman
was sacrificed not to Moloch but to the God of Israel.
Jeremiah laments:

And they have built the high places of Topheth, which
is in the valley of the son of Hinnom, to burn their sons
and their daughters in the fire; which I commanded not,
neither came it into my mind.[17]

We have not exhausted the idolatries of Israel that
drew the fire of the prophets; but we have noted the more
pernicious. The ethical was entirely absent; the animistic,
morally degrading, was predominant. In this black night
the prophets raised their impassioned voices. They were
the trumpeters of the dawn. They ridiculed, scorned, outlawed the idols, and drove the evil spirits from the world.
They stretched a new heaven over mankind, and flashed
an enthralling vision to a people dwelling in darkness.

[15]Lods, *Israel*, pp. 88–89; 99–100; 284–89. etc.   [16]Judg. 11.

[17]Jer. 7:31. For further reference to child sacrifice in Israel, see:
Gen. 22 (This story should be read as a protest against human sacrifice
as well as a plea for faith); Ex. 22:28–29; Lev. 18:21; 20:2; Deut. 12:31;
Judg. 11:39; I Kings 6:34; II Kings 3:27; 16:3; 21:6; Isa, 57:5; Jer.
19:5; 32:35; Ezek, 16:20f.; 23:37; Micah. 6:7. See art. "Human Sacrifice" (Semitic) in *HERE*.

IV

AMOS

Let justice well up as waters,
And righteousness as a mighty stream.

Amos 5:24.

AMOS AT BETH-EL

Two MEN clashed in a verbal encounter. Hot, impassioned words rang through the sanctuary. In that collision stands dramatized the conflict between the proper, official priest and the free lance prophet; between institutional, formal religion, entrenched in the prerogatives and sanctions of the social order, and the worldly—dispossessed spirit of religion. If we view this scene, enacted by two men many centuries ago, at closer ranger we shall see the conflict between the prophet and the world.

The encounter took place about the year 750 B.C. in the royal sanctuary of Beth-el, Israel. The Temple was filled with worshippers. It must have been a colorful, happy lot, for Beth-el was a fashionable shrine. It was the king's own chapel. Men of power and affluence were there; ladies of leisure and social standing were there. The Temple was an ancient shrine, the nest of a time-honored tradition. It had "background," social prestige, the "true faith." The ecclesiastic presiding over this fashionable, successful Temple was a man by the name of

Amaziah. He is one of the two men we see in the encounter. We must view him at closer range, for in him
stands personified the established order of his day at which
the prophet hurled his denunciation.

Amaziah must have been admired by the lesser clergy
of his day, for he was the most successful of his fraternity.
He probably thought and spoke in the terms of the world
about him—conventional, proper, safe. His point of view
must have been the point of view of the society of which
he was a part; his scale of values was probably the scale
of values approved by the social register of the day. He
must have been regular in his patriotism, silent and safe
in politics, amiable of personality, ministering on the
basis of social compatibility rather than in terms of a
driving religious conviction. He was quite likely "a good
fellow," and "played the game."

This man was the spiritual leader of Beth-el at a time
when the country was enjoying an abundant prosperity.
"A generation had grown up that had not known defeat,"
writes one scholar.[1] On the throne was Jereboam II, a powerful monarch and military leader, who had cleared his
country of foreign tribes, extended its frontiers in every
direction, exacted tribute from many nations, and raised
Israel to a position of supremacy. A strutting army was
at his command. It gloried in its victories. Commercially,
too, the nation thrived and grew fat and arrogant. Across
its ample fields stretched the trade routes between Egypt
in the south and the markets of the north, and between
the fertile shores of the Mediterranean in the west and
the trans-Jordanic markets in the east. In the wake of this

[1]George Adam Smith, *The Book of the Twelve Prophets*, p. 32.

prosperity came the rise of cities and all the social ills that go with large centers of population sprung up in the wake of a rapidly-acquired wealth. No social conscience and no social intelligence was there to mitigate the social evils. A leisure class arose which, like Jeshurun, "grew fat and thick" upon the substance of an impoverished population. Poverty stalked in the wake of prosperity; social privilege went hand in hand with social misery. We shall hear vehement, impassioned protests against such a condition when we come to the utterances of the prophets. In the wake of this prosperity trailed arrogance, an intemperance of mind and a stupefication of conscience. A sense of self-sufficiency guided the nation. "Have we not by our own strength acquired horns for ourselves?" Amos quotes the powerful of his day as saying.[2]

Amaziah, the priest at Beth-el, was the representative of this social order. He, it would seem, was the child of his age who shared the view, probably honestly enough, that his was the best possible of all worlds.

We shift the spotlight to the second man in the encounter. He was a stranger who appeared unheralded and uninvited in the midst of this colorful and powerful congregation keeping holiday. His name was Amos. His dress was that of a desert wanderer. Perhaps his speech sounded a bit foreign, for he was recognized as an alien. Uninvited, unannounced, he released a verbal barrage, criticizing mercilessly the nations bordering Israel. He denounced them for their greed, their rapacity, their inhumanity, their tribal jealousies and racial hatreds. As long as he attacked these foreign countries, the people

[2]Amos 6:13.

listened, quite likely with a good deal of satisfaction, and thought the stranger to be a patriotic citizen. Did he not attack the foreigner? And is not hounding the foreigner a sure test of patriotism? But having paid his respects to the foreign nations, he turned his fire upon Israel, and Beth-el, and the very men and women who were there before him—king, general, statesman, aristocrat. Their prosperity, he told them bluntly, was founded on inhumanity. It rested on immorality and would not endure, therefore; their superiority was nothing more than provincial arrogance; their courts were dens of thieves, the poor man having no chance before the law; their temples were centers of immoral religion; their imposing ritual, their chanting and their sacrifices were an abomination unto the Lord. A nation founded on such a basis cannot exist. By the justice of God it would not exist. A fearful vision of Israel prostrate with none to save her, her pride broken, her young men and women murdered by the foe, her lords and ladies carried off into exile as slaves, flashed before him. Hot, impassioned words flew from his lips; they must have dismayed his hearers. Amaziah, spokesman for his sanctuary, could stand it no longer. Treason! treason! he cried. "The land is not able to bear all his words. . . . O thou seer, go! Flee into the land of Judah and there prophesy but prophesy not again here at Beth-el, for it is the king's sanctuary and a royal house."[3]

But Amos did not flee. He remained and spoke his mind. His words were reported in a book that bears his name. Who was Amos? What are the characteristics of his per-

[3]Amos 7:10–17.

sonality, and what the story of his life? How did the fire
of God enter his soul?

LIFE IN TEKOA

Our knowledge of his life is meager. From the opening
verse of his book, as we have it, we learn that his name
was Amos, that he gave expression to his prophecies about
the year 750 B.C., that he was "among the herdsmen of
Tekoa," and that the sheep he tended were small, stunted
animals with short legs and ugly faces. They were prized
for their wool. There may have been a settlement of these
shepherds at Tekoa; perhaps Amos was a lone figure. To
secure his meager subsistence he resorted, also, to the
dressing of sycamores, cultivating a fruit "something like
a small fig, in shape and size, but insipid and woody in
taste."[4] Tekoa was a dreary land, "a waste and howling
wilderness." George Adam Smith gives a masterful description of this waste land and suggests its effect upon
Amos: "The men of Tekoa looked out upon a desolate and
haggard world. South, west and north the view is barred
by a range of limestone hills, on one of which directly
north the grey towers of Jerusalem are hardly to be dis-
cerned from the grey mountain lines. Eastward the pros-
pect is still more desolate, but it is open; the land slopes
away for nearly eighteen miles to a depth of four thousand
feet. Of this long descent, the first step, lying immediately
below the hill of Tekoa, is a shelf of stony moorland with
the ruins of vineyards. It is the lowest ledge of the settled
life of Judæa. The eastern edge drops suddenly by broken
rocks to slopes spotted with bushes of 'retem,' the broom

[4]S. R. Driver in *CB*, Amos 8:14.

of the desert, and with patches of poor wheat. From the
foot of the slopes the land rolls away in a maze of low
hills and shallow dales, that flush green in spring, but for
the rest of the year are brown with withered grass and
scrub. This is the *Wilderness* or *Pastureland of Tekoa,*
across which by night the wild beasts howl, and by day the
blackened sites of deserted camps, with the loose cairns
that mark the nomads' graves, reveal a human life almost
as vagabond and nameless as that of the beasts. Beyond
the rolling land is Jeshimon, or Devastation—a chaos of
hills, none of whose ragged crests are tossed as high as the
shelf of Tekoa, while their flanks shudder down some
further thousands of feet, by crumbling precipices and
corries choked with debris, to the coast of the Dead Sea.
The northern half of this is visible, bright blue against
the red wall of Moab, and the level top of the wall, broken
only by the valley of the Arnon, constitutes the horizon. Except for the blue water—which shines in its gap
between the torn hills like a bit of sky through rifted
clouds—it is a very dreary world. Yet the sun breaks
over it, perhaps all the more gloriously; mists, rising from
the sea simmering in its great vat, drape the nakedness
of the desert noon; and through the dry desert night
the planets ride with a majesty they cannot assume in our
more troubled atmosphere. It is also a very empty and a
very silent world, yet every stir of life upon it excites,
therefore, the greater vigilance, and man's faculties, re-
lieved from the rush and confusion of events, form the
instinct of marking, and reflecting upon, every single
phenomenon. And it is a very savage world. Across it all,

the towers of Jerusalem give the only signal of the spirit, the one token that man has a history.

"Upon this unmitigated wilderness, where life is reduced to poverty and danger; where nature starves the imagination, but excites the faculties of perception and curiosity; with the mountain tops and the sunrise in his face, but above all with Jerusalem so near,—Amos did the work which made him a man, heard the voice of God calling to him to be a prophet, and gathered those symbols and figures in which his prophet's message still reaches us with so fresh and so austere an air."[5]

An occasional visit to the market places, a chance meeting with a traveller must have given Amos his understanding of the life of Judah and Israel. Brooding upon the social evils as he understood them, sensitive, spiritually vibrant as he was, and living as he did in an environment that quickened his perception and forced introspection, Amos heard the compelling voice of God. It came as an overwhelming power. "The Lord took me from following the flock, and the Lord said unto me: Go, prophesy unto My people Israel."[6] Amos was in the grip of a power beyond himself.

AMOS DENOUNCES THE NATIONS

The Lord roareth from Zion,
His voice thundereth from Jerusalem;
And the habitations of the shepherd shall mourn,
And the top of Carmell shall wither.[7]

[5]George Adam Smith, *The Book of the Twelve Prophets,* pp. 74–76, (Harper & Brothers, publishers).
[6]Amos 7:15.   [7]Amos 1:2.

Thus does Amos begin his address, as preserved in the first two chapters of the book of Amos. The wrath of a just God is sure to fall upon the sinful nations. Sure, swift, merciless will be the visitation of God. Out of Zion, where stands His earthly habitation, His word shall go forth and all the earth shall wilter. In swift procession the cruel nations of the world pass before the righteous Judge of all the earth and receive staggering sentences. Damascus had invaded a neighboring state and tortured an innocent population with "sledges of iron"; therefore the sword shall fall upon Damascus and fire shall raze her palaces. Philistia trafficked in slaves, growing fat and mighty by feeding the slave markets of the world; therefore her proud cities must sink into ruins and her inhabitants perish. Tyre, the opulent city of the North, "the mart of the nations," as Isaiah called her, into whose lap emptied all the trade routes by land and by sea, drew her prosperity from the broken bodies of slaves; she was the auction-block of the nations; therefore Tyre must fall and her prosperity be swept away. Edom plundered her neighbors with a merciless sword, showing no pity; therefore Edom must sink into ruins. The Ammonites ripped open the pregnant women of a neighboring nation in their mad military pursuits; therefore Ammon must fall and rise no more. Moab is revengeful, unrelenting in her savage hatred of a neighboring nation; therefore a merciless destruction shall befall Moab.

Thus the prophet surveys the nations, summons them before the Lord of all, and pronounces staggering sentences.

The indictment of the nations was only his introduction.

Before the bar of divine justice he summoned his own
Judah and the sister state, Israel, where he spoke. Judah
is faithless to her God; sham religion is crowding out the
true worship of God. "Their lies have caused them to
err." Jerusalem will therefore mourn in her ashes. Finally,
Amos concentrates his wrath on Israel. The sins of Israel
are severe: justice is perverted, the poor are exploited,
immorality and self-indulgence are rampant in the land,
practised in the very sanctuaries of God. The Day of the
Lord will therefore come, "and it will be an evil time."

"HEAR YE THIS WORD"

Amos continues his attack on Israel with what may be
considered three distinct addresses, each beginning with
the phrase, "Hear ye this word."[8] The central thought
is that catastrophe hangs over the nation. A society that
violates the will of God cannot endure. Collapse is inevitable. His invective against the nobility, the wealthy,
the priesthood, the ladies of society—whom he calls "cows
of Bashan"—is bitter and excited. Before him flashes a
black vision: Israel lies prostrate, her beauty ravished, her
strength gone, her doom sealed. He chants a dirge over
the nation:

Hear ye this word which I take up—
    a dirge, O house of Israel.

Fallen is the virgin of Israel;
No more shall she rise!
Prostrate she lies on the ground,
None is there to raise her up!

[8]3; 4; 5–6.

For thus saith the Lord God:
The city that sent forth a thousand shall have a hundred
    left; and the city that sent forth a hundred shall
    have but ten left, for the house of Israel.

For thus saith the Lord to the house of Israel:
Seek Me and live;
But seek not Beth-el,
Cross not over to Beer-sheba;
For Gilgal shall go into exile,
And Beth-el, house of God, shall become vanity.[9]

Seek the Lord and live,
Lest He break forth like fire, O House of Joseph,
And it devour, and there be none to quench at Beth-el.

Ah! He that maketh the Seven Stars and the Orion,
And turneth the blackest darkness into morning,
And darkeneth the day into night;
That calleth for the waters of the sea,
And poureth them out on the face of the earth;
The Lord is His name!

He it is that causeth destruction to fall upon the strong,
And bringeth devastation upon the fortress.

Ye that turn justice to wormwood,
And cast righteousness to the ground!

They hate him that reproveth in the gate,
And abhor him who speaketh uprightly.

Therefore, because ye trample upon the poor,
And take exactions of wheat from him

[9]George Adam Smith, in *Book of the Twelve Prophets,* pp. 165–6,
suggests "And Beth-El, house of God, shall go to the devil."

Though ye have built houses of hewn stones,
Ye shall not dwell in them;
Though ye have planted pleasant vineyards,
Ye shall not drink the wine thereof.

For I know how manifold are your crimes,
And how mighty are your sins—
Ye that browbeat the righteous, take bribes,
And defeat the poor in the gates.

Therefore the prudent shall keep silent in such a time,
For it shall be an evil time.

Seek good and not evil, that ye may live;
And so the Lord, the God of hosts, may be with you, as
     ye say.

Hate evil and love good;
Set justice on her feet again in the gates.
Perhaps the Lord God will have mercy upon the remnant
     of Joseph.

Therefore thus saith the Lord, the God of hosts:
Lamentations shall be heard in all the broad places,
And they shall be saying in all streets, "Woe! Woe!"
And they shall call the husbandman to mourning,
And to lamentation all them that are skilful in dirges.

Wailing shall be heard in every vineyard,
For I will pass through the midst of thee, saith the Lord.[10]

The thought was deeply imbedded in the minds of the
masses and their leaders that a day would eventually
come when Israel would rise triumphant over all its foes.

[10]5:1–17.

God Himself would crush the enemies of Israel and lavish
His boundless gifts upon His own. That great day would
be the Day of the Lord. Amos, too, looked to the Day of
the Lord; but he gave it a new and, to his hearers, a
shocking meaning. The Day of the Lord would be for
Israel not a day of triumph and glory, but a day of
judgment and defeat:

Woe unto you that desire the day of the Lord!
Wherefore would ye have the day of the Lord?
It is darkness, and not light.
As if a man did flee from a lion,
And a bear met him!
Or went into the house and leaned his hand on the wall
And a serpent bit him!
Shall not the day of the Lord be darkness, and no light?
Even very dark, and no brightness in it?[11]

Ritual will not save them, for ritual is abhorrent to
God when it becomes a substitute for ethical religion.

I hate, I despise your feasts,
And I will take no delight in your solemn assemblies.
Yea, though ye offer me burnt-offerings and your meal-
offerings,
I will not accept them;
Neither will I regard the meal-offerings of your fat beasts.
Take thou away from me the noise of thy songs;
And let Me not hear the melodies of thy psalteries.
But let justice well up as waters,
And righteousness as a mighty stream.[12]

He is the God of justice who wants not mere ritual
but just relationships between a man and his neighbor.
It was not ritual as such to which Amos—and the rest of

[11]5:18–20. Tr. by George Adam Smith, *ibid.*   [12]5:21–24.

the prophets—objected; what he objected to was ritual without moral character and social justice.

Here Amos reaches his grand climax:

> Let justice well up as waters,
> And righteousness as a mighty stream.

Not national conceit, not ritual, not sacrifices and not chants, but justice is the will of God.

VISIONS

The last three chapters of the book of Amos are a series of visions—rapid, vivid, daring. They repeat the prophet's burden that doom is cracking over the head of the nation. Devouring locusts, sweeping fire, God standing upon a wall with plumbline in hand gauging the justice of the national structure, a basket of ripe fruit silently testifying to the nation's ripeness for judgment, the sanctuary trembling to its foundations and sagging under the impact—all these point to the day when the people of Israel "shall wander from sea to sea, and from the dark north to the sunrise shall they run to and fro, to seek the word of the Lord, and they shall not find it. . . ."[13]

THE GREATNESS AND THE WEAKNESS OF AMOS

Little hope to relieve the gloom, little faith in the God of mercy, who forgives and heals because of His infinite compassion, no trace of cheer, no inkling of a sense of humor—a grave fault which Amos shared with the rest of the prophets—no doubt in his own convictions mitigates the pronouncements of Amos. Hard, harsh, mercilessly

[13] 8:12. Tr. by George Adam Smith.

dogmatic, he hurls denunciation at an unjust society and its flunkies. Uncompromising justice—that is the greatness and the weakness of Amos. He did not know what the later rabbis knew, that the world cannot endure on the basis of justice alone; hence God tempered justice with mercy. The embrace of justice and mercy preserves the world.

> God is the Lord of the universe. It is He
> . . . that maketh the Pleiades and Orion,
> And bringeth on the shadow of death in the morning,
> And darkeneth the day into night;
> That calleth for the waters of the sea,
> And poureth them out upon the face of the earth;
> The Lord is His name.[14]

He is the God of all the nations; all nations must obey His will. The wrongs against which Amos storms are violations of the moral law, not merely violations of custom or ritual. And he speaks not as a provincial patriot; he does not restrict his censure to wrongs done to Israel. Basic human decency is what he defends. Righteousness is the will of God; righteousness is the foundation of the world. Thus does Amos lift the religion of Israel from the ritualistic and the national to the ethical and universal. George Adam Smith gives a spirited summary of the thought of Amos: "To him, unlike his fellows, unlike especially Hosea, the whole land is one theatre of judgment; but it is a theatre trembling to its foundations with the drama enacted upon it. Nay, land and nature are themselves actors in the drama. Physical forces are inspired with moral purpose, and become ministers of right-

[14]Amos 5:8.

eousness. . . . Therefore Amos was driven to show that nature and morality are one. Morality is not a set of conventions. 'Morality is the order of things.' Righteousness is on the scale of the universe. All things tremble to the shock of sin; all things work together for good to them that fear God."[15]

[15]*Book of the Twelve Prophets,* pp. 200–201.

V

HOSEA

And I will betroth thee unto Me forever;
Yea, I will betroth thee unto Me in righteousness and justice,
And in lovingkindness and in compassion;
I will betroth thee unto Me in faithfulness,
And thou shalt know the Lord.

HOSEA 2:21–22 (19–20).

A PROPHET'S MARRIAGE

SOME ten to fifteen years after Amos' appearance at Beth-el a new voice was raised in Israel. It was a voice of basic justice, tender mercy, deep compassion, loving-kindness, long-suffering. From a heart heavy with grief came this pleading voice—pleading for regeneration and a "return to the Lord."

Sow to yourselves according to righteousness,
Reap according to mercy,
Break up your fallow ground;
For it is time to seek the Lord,
Till He come and cause righteousness to rain upon you.
Ye have plowed wickedness, ye have reaped iniquity,
Ye have eaten the fruit of lies;
For thou didst trust in thy chariots,
In the multitude of thy mighty men.[1]

[1]Hos. 10:12–13. "In thy chariots," see Cheney, *CB* on 10:13.

Hosea was a native of Israel, the only one of the Hebrew literary prophets to come from that country. He lived and preached in his native land. His whole life, his every experience was bound up with the fate of his land and his people. Scholars place his activity as a prophet between the years 750 and 735 B.C. He was a man of sorrow; his message to his own people—and to a sinning, suffering humanity the world over to this day—sprang from his broken heart. Like all his colleagues, he was an alien among his own people, an outcast in his own native community. He must have been scorned and derided. "The prophet is distracted, the man of the spirit is crazed," he complains, because of the corruption into which his people have fallen. "The prophet—the fowler's snare is upon all his ways; opposition is in the house of his God. They have dug a deep pit for him. . . ."[2] Despite the intensely subjective manner of his teaching, we know but little of the facts of his life. His strange, unhappy marriage is reported in the first and third chapters of the book that bears his name.

Do these chapters report one event in the life of the prophet or two different stages in his life? Are the chapters supplementary or contradictory? Is it the same woman who figures in the two chapters? And is the story reported an allegory or a fact?

The story of his marriage seems to be as follows:[3] Harassed by the moral corruption about him, Hosea was driven to marry a known prostitute. Her name was Gomer bath Diblaim. Translated, *bath diblaim* means, "daughter

---

[2] 9:7–9. J. M. Powis Smith tr.
[3] See J. M. Powis Smith, *The Prophet and His Problems,* Chap. 5.

of fig-cakes"—that is, "Gomer-not-worth-a-fig." He did
not court her to win her love; he bought her from her
paramour, as one bought a slave in those days. He paid
for her fifteen pieces of silver and one and a half homer
of barley. The price is estimated at thirty shekels, some
ten dollars. That was probably the average price of a
slave. He subjected her to a period of restraint. He would
refine and redeem her with his boundless pity, self-sacri-
fice, and love. But she persistently relapsed into her moral
lewdness. Three children were born to them. They are
described as "children of whoredom." They were of doubtful paternity. He gave them symbolic names. His first-
born, a son, he called Jezreel; his second child, a daughter,
he named Lo-ruhamah; his second son he called Lo-ammi.

These names were striking in their meanings, even as
the marriage itself was. Jezreel was the battleground of
ancient Israel. There, a hundred and twenty-five years
earlier, King Ahab's family was murdered, and Israel
never forgot the horrid experience. There Israel would
meet its fate again, Hosea was convinced, for the judgment of God would befall the nation as it did in the days
of idolatrous King Ahab. Lo-ruhamah means, "She-who-
is-unpitied"; Lo-ammi means, "Not-my-people." His children were walking sermons, dramatizing the impending
doom hanging over the nation; inevitable judgment, final
alienation, complete rejection!

What explains this marriage is the prophet's burning
desire to arouse his people to a realization of their in-
fidelity to their God and the inevitable consequences. He
hoped thereby to startle Israel into a realization of its
idolatrous and adulterous conduct as the people of God.

It was an object-lesson. By it Hosea meant to dramatize the existing situation between God and Israel. Like Gomer, Israel was disloyal and ungrateful—this despite God's infinite compassion.

> Israel is stubborn like a stubborn heifer . . .

> O Ephraim, thou hast committed harlotry,
> Israel is defiled.

> Ephraim is wedded to idols;
> Let him alone.[4]

Of what avail is it to talk reason and duty and honor with a people drunk with an evil passion? Nevertheless, he pleads and hopes:

> Plead with your mother, plead;
> For she is not My wife, neither am I her husband;
> And let her put away her harlotries from her face,
> And her adulteries from between her breasts;
> Lest I strip her naked,
> And set her as in the day that she was born,
> And make her as a wilderness,
> And set her like a dry land,
> And slay her with thirst.
> And I will not have compassion upon her children;
> For they are children of harlotry.
> For their mother hath played the harlot,
> She that conceived them hath done shamefully;
> For she said: "I will go after my lovers,
> That give me my bread and my water,
> My wool and my flax, mine oil and my drink."[5]

[4]4:16; 5:3; 4:17; Ephraim, *i.e.,* Israel.
[5]Hos. 2:4–7 (2–5).

INVASION—ASSASSINATION—DISRUPTION

Hosea lived in a noisy, chaotic age. The plundering invader was loose in the world. Social decay, economic injustice, religious degeneracy were rampant in his native land. Ten to fifteen years earlier, when Amos chanted his dirge over Israel, the country was prosperous; the masses and their leaders felt safe. God was in Beth-el, and Jereboam II was on the throne. In the days of Hosea, however, Israel was on a toboggan. The prophet saw nothing but a black chasm below—unless the masses and their leaders experienced a new heart and returned to the Lord.

Jereboam II was still on the throne; but the "Indian summer" of his reign—as this stretch in the history of Israel has been described—was about ended. The skies were growing heavy. Raw winds from the north were sweeping down upon the land, soon to lay it prostrate.

Hosea saw the opening scenes of national disruption and collapse. He saw in it the hand of God because of the sins of His people.

But God is a God of love. His loving-kindness redeems and restores. That was Hosea's central thought. He could not bring himself to believe that God would abandon His own. The tender compassion of the prophet, his faith in a God of mercy, his hope against hope is eloquently expressed in one of the chapters of his book:

How shall I give thee up, Ephraim?
How shall I surrender thee, Israel?
How shall I make thee as Admah?
How shall I set thee as Zeboim?
My heart is turned within Me,

My compassions are kindled together.
I will not execute the fierceness of Mine anger,
I will not return to destroy Ephraim;
For I am God, and not man,
The Holy One in the midst of thee,
And I will not come in fury.
They shall walk after the Lord.
Who shall roar like a lion;
For He shall roar,
And the children shall come trembling from the west,
They shall come trembling as a bird out of Egypt,
And as a dove out of the land of Assyria;
And I will make them to dwell in their houses,
Saith the Lord.[6]

But the gloomy prophet's gloomiest forebodings came
true. Israel never returned "like a dove out of the land
of Assyria." Israel went into Assyria like a foolish lamb
and was slaughtered.

"THE LORD HATH A CONTROVERSY"

The moral and religious life of Israel is pictured in
dismal colors by Hosea. Behind the conditions he condemns are two basic causes. Hosea seems to have been
unaware of them.

First, by Hosea's time cities had developed in Israel.
Large centers of population had sprung up in the wake
of successful wars. The trade routes between Egypt and
Babylonia, Phœnicia and Arabia, passed through the
broad and fertile valleys of northern Israel. The agricultural and pastoral felt the disturbance of the com-

[6]11:8–11. Admah, Zeboim, like Sodom and Gomorrah, were cities destroyed forever because of their moral corruption.

mercial. With large centers of population came many
social problems.

Second, a wealthy, exploiting nobility arose. "Wealth
accumulated and men decayed." The middle class was
largely depleted by the many wars and revolutions; many
were reduced to serfdom. The ancient evil ran its vicious
circle: the poor grew poorer and the rich richer. The large
landowners were crowding out the small farmer. The government, the courts, the sanctuaries came into the hands
of the rich.

Hosea gives us a vivid picture of the moral and religious
conditions of his time:

Hear the word of the Lord, ye children of Israel!
For the Lord hath a controversy with the inhabitants of
    the land,
Because there is no truth, nor mercy,
Nor knowledge of God in the land.
(There is nothing but) perjury and lying, and robbery
    and murder and adultery and constant violence and
    bloodshed.[7]

The blame lies not with the people but with their spiritual
leaders:

Let none find fault and none upbraid;
For my people are but as their priestlings.
O priest, thou hast stumbled today;
And stumble tonight shall the priests with thee.[8]

My people are destroyed for lack of knowledge;
Because thou hast rejected knowledge,

[7] 4:1-2.
[8] 4:4. Tr. by George Adam Smith, *Book of the Twelve Prophets,* p. 257.

I will also reject thee, that thou shalt be no priest to Me;
Seeing thou hast forgotten the law of thy God,
I also will forget thy children.[9]

The priests thrive and grow fat on the vice of the day;
they are silent partners in its traffic. Hosea flings a burning indictment:

They eat the sin-offering of My people,
And set their heart on their iniquity.
And it is like people, like priest;
And I will punish him for his ways,
And will recompense him his doings.
And they shall eat, and not have enough,
They shall commit harlotry, and shall not increase;
Because they have left off to take heed to the Lord.[10]

The effects of a degenerate priesthood upon the people
is appalling:

Harlotry, wine, and new wine take away the heart.
My people ask counsel at their stock,
And their staff declareth unto them;
For the spirit of harlotry hath caused them to err,
And they have gone astray from under their God.
They sacrifice upon the tops of mountains,
And offer upon the hills,
Under oaks and poplars and terebinths,
Because the shadow thereof is good;
Therefore your daughters commit harlotry,
And your daughters-in-law commit adultery.
I will not punish your daughters when they commit
    harlotry,
Nor your daughters-in-law when they commit adultery;
For they themselves consort with lewd women,

[9]4:6.   [10]4:8–11. "Sin-offering," see *CB* to this verse.

And they sacrifice with harlots;
And the people that is without understanding must come
　　to ruin.[11]

The "harlots" referred to were the holy prostitutes
kept in the temples. They were consecrated prostitutes
dedicated to the service of Ashera or of Ashtoreth.[12]

Such was the priesthood of the time. To see it in all
its moral misery we need but to recall, by contrast, the
description of the faithful priest, as given by another
prophet:

> The law of truth was in his mouth,
> And unrighteousness was not found in his lips;
> He walked with Me in peace and uprightness,
> And did turn many away from iniquity.
> For the priest's lips should keep knowledge,
> And they should seek the law at his mouth;
> For he is the messenger of the Lord of hosts.[13]

But perhaps we should make allowances for Hosea's
report of the conditions of his time. Prophets and reformers are given to exaggeration. Objectivity is not
their virtue. The prophets were not neutral reporters of
events. What they saw and what they spoke came with all
the fire of their divinely-gifted natures. Overstatement
was, therefore, inevitable.

"A DOOR OF HOPE"

Unlike Amos, Hosea never lost hope for his people,
for he had faith in the loving-kindness of God. A vision

[11]4:11–14.　　　　[12]See Chap. 3.　　　　[13]Mal. 2:6–7.

of moral rehabilitation and reconciliation dispelled the
gloom. God's infinite love must redeem and reclaim. With
everlasting love will He restore them and with tender
mercy will He consecrate them. God is not a man that He
should be angry forever. He will be as the dew unto
Israel, and Irael "shall blossom as the lily and cast forth
his roots like Lebanon." God is love and love is the great
redeemer, healer, and restorer:

Therefore, behold, I will allure her,
And bring her into the wilderness,
And speak tenderly to her.
And I will give back her vineyards there,
And the valley of Troubling as a door of hope;
And she shall respond there, as in the days of her youth,
And as in the day when she came up out of the land of
    Egypt.

And it shall be at that day, saith the Lord,
That thou shall call Me Ishi (my husband),
And shalt call Me no more Baali (my Baal).
For I will take the names of the Baalim out of her mouth,
And they shall no more be mentioned by their name.
And in that day will I make a covenant for them
With the beasts of the field and the fowls of heaven,
And with the creeping things of the ground;
And I will break the bow and the sword and the battle
    out of the land,
And will make them to lie down safely.

And I will betroth thee unto Me forever;
Yea, I will betroth thee unto Me in righteousness and
    justice,
And in lovingkindness, and in compassion.

And I will betroth thee unto Me in faithfulness;
And thou shalt know the Lord.
And it shall come to pass in that day,
I will respond, saith the Lord; I will respond to the
    heavens,
And they shall respond to the earth;
And the earth shall respond to the corn and the wine
    and the oil;
And they shall respond to Jezreel (whom God soweth).
And I will sow her unto Me in the land;
And I will have compassion upon her that had not ob-
    tained compassion;
And I will say to them that were not My people, "Thou
    art My people,"
And they shall say, "Thou art my God."[14]

Hosea was probably unaware of the growing pain the
religion of Israel was experiencing in his day. He did not
understand that the idolatries he denounced represented
a natural and inevitable process of assimilation. The desert
God the Israelites had brought into Canaan—which Hosea
idealizes and transforms by the sensitiveness of his own
great heart—and the local agricultural Baalim were in a
process of fusion. The nomadic Israelites were becoming
agriculturists. They were growing in a new habit of life
and in a new frame of mind. The idolatries Hosea denounced were part of the agricultural endeavor; the religion of the Canaanitish farmer was bound up with seed
time and harvest, with rain, wind, cloud, sunshine, fertility,
drought. The desert deity was an alien in this setting.
Gradually he was transformed. Hosea did not realize that

[14]2:16–25 (14–23). *The wilderness*, *i.e.*, the earliest stage in Israel's history; hence, Hosea represents God as restoring Israel to the nobility of
its youth.

he himself was doing heroic work in transforming him. He was giving new content to old forms.

HOSEA AND AMOS

Hosea presents a striking contrast to Amos and, in the end, supplements him. Amos thunders the stern, unbending justice and wrath of God; Hosea pleads, exhorts, and woos in the name of the loving-kindness of God. Amos is concerned with man's inhumanity to man; Hosea is absorbed with man's disloyalty to God. Amos objected to the cultus of the time as a substitute for justice; Hosea objected to it as a misrepresentaion of God. Amos has hardly a word of hope for his nation; Hosea pleads for regeneration, for God will forgive and save. Their forms of expression are in contrast. The book of Amos is vivid, flashing, daring in imagery; the sentences are rounded and climax leads to climax. The book of Hosea is incoherent, entirely lacking in form; the imagery is subdued, the phrases are abrupt. "Whilst in Amos the ethical element entirely predominates, in Hosea the religious element occupies the foreground. He and his intellectual and spiritual compcer, Jeremiah, were men of emotion, the most intense and the most deeply religious of all the prophets of Israel."[15]

But the two men supplement and complete each other. Justice is the groundwork of the social order; it is the primary principle in regulating man's relationship to man. But it is not adequate; it must be supplemented by what Hosea—and the later rabbinic masters—called lovingkindness. The rabbinic sages bring Amos and Hosea into

[15]C. H. Cornill, *The Prophets of Israel*, p. 48.

one harmonious whole. "When the Creator, blessed be His name," they say, "saw that man could not endure if measured by the attributes of strict justice, He joined His attribute of mercy to that of justice, and created man by the combined principle of both."[16]

[16]*Genesis Rabbah*, 8:4-5.

VI

ISAIAH

Holy, holy, holy is the Lord of hosts;
The whole earth is full of His glory.

They shall not hurt nor destroy
In all My holy mountain;
For the earth shall be full of the
  knowledge of the Lord,
As the waters cover the sea.

Isaiah 6:3; 11:9.

"THE VISION OF ISAIAH"

THE FIRST chapter of the book of Isaiah may be read as a prologue to the prophecies of Isaiah, prince of the prophets, who, perhaps more than any other of the inspired figures of Hebrew prophecy, brought the fire of heaven down to earth. Whatever the reason that led the compilers of the book to place this chapter first, it serves as an admirable prelude to the flaming scroll that holds the words of Isaiah. It begins with the words, "The vision of Isaiah. . . ." Let us commune with this vision before venturing any further; let us allow it to pass through our minds and quicken our imagination. The spirit and the power of the prophet are in it.

God has a controversy with His people, Israel. Israel is ignorant, ungrateful, disloyal. In bold, vivid terms, the prophet represents God as taking His stand to press

charges against His people; heaven and earth are called
to testify.

> Hear, O heavens, and give ear, O earth,
> For the Lord hath spoken;
> Children I have reared and exalted
> And they have rebelled against Me.
> The ox knoweth his owner
> And the ass his master's crib;
> But Israel doth not know,
> My people doth not consider.[1]

The prophet takes up the cry. Israel is a sinful nation;
a brood of evil-doers. The visitations of God have fallen
heavily upon the land; it has been reduced to a lump of
wounds and bruises and "putrefying sores." Plundered
and desolate, the land is deserted. But it is of no avail.
Israel remains blindly rebellious. At the core of the tragedy
is immoral religion. The prophet unleashes his wrath
against a religion that exhausts itself in ritual. In ringing words—strangely reminiscent of Amos—Isaiah condemns the religion of his people because in it the ceremonial
has replaced the moral.

Hear the word of the Lord,
Ye rulers of Sodom;
Give ear unto the instruction of our God
Ye people of Gomorrah.
To what purpose is the multitude of your sacrifices unto
　　Me?
Saith the Lord.
I am sated with the burnt offerings of rams
And the fat of fed beasts;
And I delight not in the blood of bullocks,

[1]1:2–3.

Or of lambs, or of he-goats.
When ye come to appear before Me,
Who hath required this at your hands?
Trample my courts no more,
Bring offerings no more.
Vain is the smoke of sacrifice,
It is an abomination unto Me.
New moon and sabbath, the calling of assemblies,—
I cannot endure iniquity and solemn meeting.
Your new moons and your appointed feasts
My soul hateth.
They are a burden unto Me;
I am weary to hear them.
And when ye spread forth your hands,
I will hide My eyes from you.
Yea, when ye make many prayers,
I will not hear:
Your hands are full of blood.
Wash you, make you clean;
Put away the evil of your doings
From before Mine eyes;
Cease to do evil:
Learn to do well;
Seek justice,
Restrain the oppressor,
Judge the fatherless,
Plead for the widow.[2]

No vague abstractions, no nice definitions of religion, no fine speculations as to what is the will of God, but an intense moral passion concentrated on a specific moral evil spells the genius of Hebrew prophecy.

Sacrifice, ritual, and prayer have their places in religion; but the first demand of the prophet is an aroused

2 1:10–17.

conscience. There must be, further, reason. Isaiah expresses a daring thought. God pleads with man to be reasonable and just:

> Come now, let us reason together,
> Saith the Lord;
> If your sins be as scarlet
> Can they become white as snow?
> If they be red like crimson,
> Can they become as wool?
> If ye be willing and obedient,
> Ye shall eat the good of the land:
> But if ye refuse and rebel,
> Ye shall be devoured with the sword.
> For the mouth of the Lord hath spoken it.[3]

But far from being reasonable and just, Jerusalem, the once faithful, once holy city has turned prostitute. Isaiah condemns in scathing terms the city he loves with all the passion of his great heart, and chants a dirge over it, even as did Amos:

How is the faithful city
Become an harlot!
She that was full of justice!
Righteousness lodged in her,
But now murderers.
Thy silver is become dross,
Thy wine adulterated with water.
Thy rulers are unruly
And companions of thieves.
Every one loveth bribes
And followeth after rewards:
They judge not the fatherless
Neither doth the cause of the widow come unto them.

[3] 1:18–20.

Therefore saith the Lord, the Lord of hosts,
The Mighty One of Israel,
Ah, I will appease Me of Mine adversaries,
And avenge Me of Mine enemies;
And I will turn My hand against thee,
And will purge thy dross as with lye
And will remove all thy alloy.
And I will restore thy judges as at the first,
And thy counsellors as at the beginning.
Afterwards thou shalt be called the City of Righteousness,
The Faithful City.[4]

In time, righteous men—however few in number—will recapture Jerusalem's ancient idealism and convert her from a prostitute city into a faithful community. This hope Isaiah never lost, however dark the skies above him, however chaotic, mad, and bloody the life about him.

Who was this man who spoke with such strange, impassioned eloquence? Where and when did he live? What was the moral atmosphere of his age? What convictions possessed him?

His life was tangled up with the life of his beloved Jerusalem and Judah; this, in turn, was enmeshed in the shifting world-forces of the time. Before we can envisage the personality of Isaiah, we must grasp the main facts in the life about him.

THE WORLD OF ISAIAH

The dominant fact in the world of Isaiah was Assyria, the terror from the north. In 745 B.C. Tiglath-pileser IV came to the throne of Assyria. He was one of the most ruthless conquerors and ablest organizers that land of

[4] 1:21–26.

plundering conquerors had produced. For eighteen years
he terrorized the world about him, invading city after city
as he pushed his way southward, plundering the nests of
civilization. Isaiah gives voice to the spirit of the invader;
he represents him as saying:

By the strength of my hand I have done it,
And by my wisdom, for I am prudent;
In that I have removed the bounds of the peoples,
And have robbed their treasures,
And have brought down as one mighty the inhabitants;
And my hand hath found as a nest the riches of the
    peoples;
And as one gathereth eggs that are forsaken
Have I gathered all the earth;
And there was none that moved his wing,
Or that opened the mouth, or chirped.[5]

    The invader penetrated as far south as Ashdod and
captured the throne of Philistia.

    Tiglath-pileser introduced a new policy in dealing with
conquered peoples. The earlier policy had been to exact
heavy tribute but to retain the native rulers; the new
policy was to appoint Assyrian governors. The conqueror's
grip upon the vanquished provinces was all the firmer.
Moreover, whole peoples were deported and scattered
among the far-flung provinces of Assyria. The purpose of
this was to mix the subjugated peoples and thus completely undo their tribal or national loyalties. It is this
policy that undid the "Ten Lost Tribes of Israel."

    Israel lay helpless before the marauding Assyrian
legions. It was badly disrupted by internal strife. Upon

[5]10:13–14.

the death of Jereboam II in 745 B.C. a period of anarchy ensued. "In fourteen years there were six kings of Israel, four of whom were assassinated and one captured in battle, while only one was succeeded by a son."[6]

About the year 738 Assyria invaded Israel. On the precarious throne of Israel was Menahem, assassin and usurper. Perhaps he welcomed the invasion as a means of bolstering up his own position. The biblical historian reports:

There came against the land Pul the king of Assyria; and Menahem gave Pul a thousand talents of silver, that his hand might be with him to confirm the kingdom in his hand. And Menahem exacted the money of Israel, even of all the mighty men of wealth, of each man fifty shekels of silver, to give to the king of Assyria. So the king of Assyria turned back, and stayed not there in the land.[7]

That was an enormous tribute. The money was raised by direct taxation. Some sixty thousand proprietors were taxed fifty shekels each. Menahem managed to maintain himself on the throne of Israel for ten years longer, but a strong anti-Assyrian party developed. His son, who succeeded him as king, was a puppet in the hands of Assyria. He was king for about a year when he was murdered by the leader of the anti-Assyrian party, Pekah by name, who seized the throne. Shortly after that, the assassin was himself assassinated and a new assassin was on the throne of Israel.

In the year 735 B.C. Syria and Israel entered into an alliance to invade Judah. The purpose was probably to

---

[6]Bailey and Kent, *History of the Hebrew Commonwealth*, p. 192.
[7]II Kings 15:19–20.

coerce Judah into a coalition against Assyria. The relationship between Judah and the sister state had been none too happy. General hostility, rivalry, hatred, open warfare characterized their relationships from the day Israel seceded from Judah in the year 933 B.C. Judah was hard-pressed. It faced a major crisis. King Ahaz was inclined to turn directly to Assyria for assistance. That was a grave step, fraught with danger. At this juncture in the destiny of the nation the figure of Isaiah emerges.

A fragmentary report of an interview Isaiah had with King Ahaz is given in chapters VII–VIII of the book of Isaiah. The prophet's mind in this crucial hour of decision for his nation is reasonably well revealed. The prophet seeks to reassure the harassed king. The "two tales of smoking firebrands," as he contemptuously describes the kings of Syria and Israel, will burn themselves out and will exhaust themselves. Nothing will come of their plans; nothing possibly can come, for they have no higher origin than the minds of two weak and noisy men. Isaiah urges signs of God's will in the matter, but the king refuses to traffic with deity. Within a few years, Isaiah insists, women will be naming their children after the great deliverance that God shall bring to Judah.[8] He was opposed to calling in the Assyrian tiger to help subdue the two fighting cats. That would be jumping from the frying pan into the fire. Assyria would become a menace to Judah, not its savior. Moreover, Isaiah was probably opposed to calling in Assyria on religious grounds. That would indicate lack of faith in God. "If

---

[8]This is the meaning of the much-discussed Emmanuel sign in Isaiah 7:14–17. See S. R. Driver, *CB,* and G. B. Gray, *ICC* to this passage.

you have no faith, you shall not be established," is his final warning. That is the light the prophet released to a people walking in darkness.

King Ahaz rejected Isaiah's advice and invited Assyrian help. Tiglath-pileser accepted only too gladly, invaded Damascus and conquered it, slew the king of Syria, and carried off large numbers of the population. Then he swept southward as far as Gaza on the Mediterranean. Israel was reduced to an Assyrian province. Only Samaria was spared the horrors of siege. The reason for that was that an Assyrian puppet was on the throne. The rest of the country was depopulated. When, upon the death of Tiglath-pileser, Israel sought to regain its independence, Assyria replied with a vigorous invasion. Samaria was besieged. For two years the city held out but finally, in the year 721, fell before Sargon's legions. That was the end of the Kingdom of Israel. "The Ten Lost Tribes" were lost forever. They were scattered in Upper Mesopotamia and Media. Samaria was settled with a mixed population. The ravenous Assyrian wolf was now next door to Judah.

About the year 720, Hezekiah came to the throne of Judah. Simultaneously, an anti-Assyrian policy was projected, reversing the policy Ahaz had followed. A change in rulers of Assyria was a signal for revolt. Judah joined Philistia, Moab, and Edom in repudiating Assyrian hegemony and turned to Egypt for assistance. Sargon, the new emperor of Assyria, responded with a swift, relentless invasion of the rebellious provinces, focusing his attack on Ashdod, Philistia, the center of anti-Assyrian insurrections.

Once again a major crisis confronted Judah, and, characteristically, once again the figure of Isaiah emerged in arresting manner. A brief biographic passage embodied in the book of Isaiah gives a vivid description of the prophet's extraordinary conduct and reveals his attitude towards the rebellion against Assyria and the flirtation with inconstant Egypt.

In the year that Tartan came unto Ashdod, when Sargon the king of Assyria sent him, and he fought against Ashdod and took it; at that time the Lord spoke by Isaiah the son of Amoz, saying: "Go, and loose the sackcloth from off thy loins, and put thy shoe from off thy foot." And he did so, walking naked and barefoot.

And the Lord said: "Like as My servant Isaiah hath walked naked and barefoot to be for three years a sign and a wonder upon Egypt and upon Ethiopia, so shall the king of Assyria lead away the captives of Egypt, and the exiles of Ethiopia, young and old, naked and barefoot, and with buttocks uncovered, to the shame of Egypt. And they shall be dismayed and ashamed, because of Ethiopia their expectation, and of Egypt their glory. And the inhabitant of this coast-land shall say in that day: Behold, such is our expectation, whither we fled for help to be delivered from the king of Assyria; and how shall we escape?"[9]

Ashdod fell before Sargon's forces in 711 B.C. Judah seems to have disentangled herself in time to save herself from Sargon's wrath.

Sargon died in 705. The hour for rebellion was rife. A change of rulers was a sure signal for revolt on the part of the subjugated peoples. Other circumstances encour-

[9]20.

aged wide rebellion. Egypt was vigorously fomenting insurrection; her ambassadors—"glossy of skin," as Isaiah described them—were active in Jerusalem. Moreover, Babylon was presenting stubborn resistance to Assyrian supremacy. On her throne was Merodach-baladan who, for twelve years, had defied and baffled the Assyrian armies. Assyria was thus preoccupied and the hour for rebellion had struck. And again Judah was in the valley of indecision.

Once again Isaiah's voice was heard. He opposed the insurrection. Assyrian power had not yet spent itself, he seems to have reasoned; moreover, the character of the terrible Sennacherib, the new emperor of Assyria, was not fully appreciated. Isaiah warned Philistia:

Rejoice not, O Philistia, all of thee,
Because the rod that smote thee is broken:
For out of the serpent's root shall come forth a basilisk,
And his fruit shall be a flying serpent.

Howl, O gate; cry, O city;
Melt away, O Philistia, all of thee;
For there cometh a smoke out of the north,
And there is no straggler in his ranks.[10]

In 701 Sennacherib lashed out against Phœnicia, Philistia, inflicting severe punishment on Egyptians and Arabs, and besieged Judah. King Hezekiah was compelled to pay indemnity and beg for mercy.[11]

Sennacherib's report of the invasion has come down to us. We must read it critically, for it is the report of a braggart.

[10]14:29–31. [11]II Kings 18:13–16.

And Hezekiah of Judah, who had not submitted to my yoke . . . 46[12] of his strongly fortified cities, and small towns in their vicinity without number; 200,150 people, young, old, male, and female, horses, mules, asses, camels, oxen, and flocks without number, I brought out from their midst, and reckoned as spoil. Himself I shut up like a caged bird in Jerusalem, his royal city.[13]

A battered fort in a wilderness was Jerusalem. The enemy was storming at her walls. King Hezekiah could do nothing but beseech the mercy of God; he begged the aged Isaiah, "lift up thy prayer for the remnant that is left." The prophet—who lived through many dark days in the life of his Jerusalem—instilled new courage in the despairing heart of his king. His advice is embodied in a superb poem.[14] He taunts the invader and chants a dirge over him; his days are numbered, for he has arrayed himself against the Holy One of Israel.

Pestilence swept through the camp. The biblical historian reports naïvely:

And the angel of the Lord went forth, and smote in the camp of the Assyrians a hundred and fourscore and five thousand; and when men arose early in the morning, behold, they were all dead corpses. So Sennacherib king of Assyria departed, and went, and returned, and dwelt at Nineveh.[15]

Sennacherib remained emperor for some twenty years longer. Judah continued paying him tribute. Never again, however, did he set foot in Palestine.

We lose sight of Isaiah in the siege and deliverance of

---

[12]It is doubtful if there were forty-six fortified cities in all of Judah.
[13]Quoted by J. Skinner, *CB* to Isaiah, p. xix.
[14]37:22b–35.   [15]37:36–37.

the year 701 B.C. The year 701 is one of the decisive dates in the history of mankind. Had Jerusalem fallen before the Assyrian invader and had the people been deported and scattered in keeping with the Assyrian policy, the moral content of civilization would have been affected to our own day and beyond. With Judea lost, as were the Ten Lost Tribes, with the voices of the prophets hushed, the moral heritage of Israel aborted, would Christianity have come into the world? Would Mohammedanism? What would the spiritual climate of these past ages have been in consequence? We lose sight of Isaiah at the moment when the shuttle is flying back and forth in the loom of time determining the moral pattern of our civilization.

THE LIFE OF ISAIAH

The life of Isaiah was inexorably bound up with the tumult, the chaos, and the faith of his age. We may now gather together the few fragmentary facts of the prophet's life.

Isaiah was a boy when Amos denounced the nations at Beth-el and demanded justice in the name of God; he was a young man when Hosea preached the compassion of God, pleading with his people to "return to the Lord." The conviction that he was called by God to be a prophet to his people must have gripped his heart about the year 740 B.C. The vision that inaugurated him as prophet is reported in superb, majestic words. Years must have passed—years of doubt and disillusionment—before he committed to writing the haunting experience of his youth.

In the year that King Uzziah died I saw the Lord sitting
upon a throne, high and lifted up, and His train filled
the temple. Above Him stood the seraphim: each one had
six wings; with twain he covered his face, and with twain
he covered his feet, and with twain he did fly. And one
cried to another and said,

> Holy, holy, holy is the Lord of hosts;
> The whole earth is full of His glory.

And the foundations of the thresholds were moved at the
voice of him that cried, and the house was filled with
smoke. Then said I,

> Woe is me! for I am undone;
> Because I am a man of unclean lips,
> And I dwell in the midst of a people of
>   unclean lips;
> For mine eyes have seen the King, the
>   Lord of hosts.

Then flew one of the seraphim unto me, having a live coal
in his hands, which he had taken with the tongs from off
the altar. He touched my mouth with it and said,

> Lo, this hath touched thy lips;
> And thine iniquity is taken away,
>   and thy sin expiated.

And I heard the voice of the Lord saying,

> Whom shall I send,
> And who will go for us?
> Then said I,
> Here am I; send me.[16]

In the year 735 B.C. we see him advising his king in
the face of the Syro-Ephraimitish invasion. He is married

[16] 6:1-8.

and has a boy by his side, who bears the name Shear-
Yashub—"a remnant will return." A year later a second
boy is born to him and receives the strange name, Maher-
Shalal-Hash-Baz—"Swift-Booty-Spoil-Prey." The same
words he inscribes on "a great tablet" and posts it where
every man may see it. Like Hosea, he gives his children
sermonic names, thus revealing his mind. The hand of
God was shaping the destiny of the world; Judah and
Jerusalem would not escape His wrath, but a remnant
would be saved—"a remnant of Jacob unto the mighty
God."

He was a citizen of Jerusalem. "More than Athens to
Demosthenes, Rome to Juvenal, Florence to Dante is
Jerusalem to Isaiah," writes George Adam Smith. "She
is his immediate and ultimate regard, the center and return of all his thoughts, the hinge of the history of his
time, the one thing worth preserving amidst its disasters,
the summit of his brilliant hopes with which he fills the
future."[17] He saw his beloved Jerusalem prostituted by
avaricious priests, princes, and elders, and he invoked
the wrath of God upon the city and its misrulers. The
conjecture among scholars is that he was of an aristocratic
family. That he was a frequent visitor at court is quite
evident from his utterances.

For some twenty years following the Syro-Ephraimitish war, when his unsolicited advice was rejected by King
Ahaz, his life is in total eclipse. Finding himself in complete disagreement with the policies his nation was following, he withdrew from the active scene. "For the Lord
spake thus to me while His hand gripped me, and in-

[17]*Isaiah,* p. 22.

structed me that I should not walk in the way of this people."[18] He committed his convictions to writing, "sealed the teaching among his disciples," and retired, "waiting for the Lord, that hideth His face from the house of Jacob, and I will hope in Him."[19] For two decades he remained silent; yet it was during this period that a momentous thing happened. The fall of Samaria and the complete collapse of northern Israel in 721 B.C. must have shaken Isaiah; but, if he enunciated any prophecies at this time, only a fragment or two have come down to us.

When he emerged from retirement, he enacted a strange scene. For three years he went about Jerusalem barefoot and practically naked. By this arresting conduct he sought to dramatize the lot of those who rebelled against Assyria, "the rod of His anger."

The date and manner of his death are unknown. Legend has it that he was sawn asunder with a wooden saw by King Manasseh.[20]

STATESMAN

If by a statesman we mean one who gives lofty and wise direction to the political life of his time rather than merely shrewd and successful manipulation of the affairs of his day, Isaiah must be regarded as a prophet-statesman. We have no suggestion that he ever held political office; whatever advice he urged upon king and people in the hours of grave decision was, for the most part, unsolicited. Moreover, his views were more often rejected than sympathetically heeded. But, unlike Amos and Hosea

[18]8:11.   [19]8:16–17.   [20]*Ascension of Isaiah,* 5:1.

before him and his younger colleague, Micah, who were content to enunciate their convictions and allow them to remain in the rarefied air of lofty prophecy, Isaiah sought to focus his prophetic views upon the immediate political issues, thus giving direction to the affairs of the day. This is one of Isaiah's chief distinctions.

Four Assyrian invasions swept Palestine during Isaiah's activity as prophet. The little land of Judah was in constant turmoil. Moral anarchy, confusion of counsel, fear, depair, and greed must have been rampant. The figure of Isaiah was like the shadow of a rock in this weary land. Subsequent events gave ample testimony to the sanity of the policies he had urged upon the nation.

When Judah faced the Syro-Ephraimitish invasion in the year 735 B.C., Isaiah pressed a policy which, to practical King Ahaz, must have seemed visionary and tantamount to surrender to disaster. The allied invaders, Isaiah urged, would speedily exhaust themselves; better to "be still and fear not," than to enter into an alliance with Assyria and thus bring an infinitely worse menace to Judah's own doors. His advice was rejected by king and people; the events that followed fully vindicated the wisdom of the prophet.[21] Twenty years later he cautioned against joining in anti-Assyrian plots; no help could be expected from Egypt. He pleaded impressively:

> Woe to the rebellious children, saith the Lord,
> That take counsel, but not of Me;
> And that form projects, but not of My spirit,
> That they may add sin to sin;

[21]Read Isaiah 8.

That walk to go down into Egypt,
And have not asked at My mouth;
To take refuge in the stronghold of Pharaoh,
And to take shelter in the shadow of Egypt![22]

The safety of the State was in the quiet acceptance of the will of God.

For thus said the Lord God, the Holy One of Israel:
In sitting still and rest shall ye be saved,
In quietness and in confidence shall be your strength;
But ye would not.[23]

To grasp his counsel, we must understand his philosophy of history, which, in turn, issues from his conception of God. Assyria was only a tool in the hands of God, Isaiah was convinced; it was "the rod of His anger," the handle of an axe God was swinging against the corrupt nations. His work done, He would discard the instrument He employed. The highest wisdom was, therefore, to obey the will of God.

It is God, "the Holy One of Israel," Who is shaping the destinies of nations. For the moment Assyria is the instrument. The ultimate goal toward which the history of Israel is moving is a redeemed, just, and holy people. Only a remnant will survive this purging process, but in this remnant lies the salvation of God. Assyria, however, drunk with her own power, does not understand her function. Her doom will therefore crash over her head.[24]

"But ye would not," Isaiah complains. His advice was

[22]30:1–2.   [23]30:15.
[24]Read 10:5–34; 14:24–27; 17:12–14; 18; 30:27–33.

rejected, and again the nation came to grief. It barely escaped the fate that befell Ashdod in 711 B.C.

The siege of Jerusalem in 701 B.C. testifies once more to Isaiah's sanity in the hour of emergency. This time his intervention was sought, more as a man of God than a statesman. His heroic faith communicated itself to the rulers and prevented the surrender of Jerusalem to Sennacherib.[25] The prophet of faith saved the city and the State.

CRITIC

The true genius of Isaiah, as of all the prophets, is best expressed in the vehement denunciation of corruption. Like whips of fire fell his words upon the smarting soul of his people. He unleashed his awful wrath against the evils of his day and no evil escaped him—ungodliness, arrogance, exploitation of the poor, concentration of wealth, crowding out the small farmer, drunkenness, corrupt courts, bragging skepticism, wilful confusion of moral values, degenerate priests, and callous, immoral women.

Perhaps we may catch something of his passion if we recall his own words. Misgovernment, cruelty, corrupt courts, immoral luxury would dissolve the bands that held society together:

And the people shall tyrannize man over man
Yea, each one over his neighbour;
The youth shall act rudely towards the old man
And the base against the honourable.[26]

[25]Read 36–37; II Kings 18:17–37; 19.   [26]3:5.

The causes for it are:

Their partiality in judgment testifies against them
And they declare their sin, like Sodom, undisguisedly.

. . . .

O my people! Babes are their masters
Women rule over them!
O my people! Your leaders mislead you
And confuse the tracks you should follow.
The Lord is taking His stand to plead,
He stands up to arraign His people
The Lord will enter into judgment
With the elders of His people, and the princes thereof:
"It is you that have devoured the vineyard—
The plunder of the poor is in your houses.
What mean ye by crushing My people
And grinding the face of the poor?"
Saith the Lord, the Lord of hosts.[27]

To the pampered ladies of society the prophet pays his
compliments:

Moreover, the Lord said,
Because the daughters of Zion are haughty,
And walk with outstretched neck
And ogling with their eyes
Mincing along as they walk
And jingling with their feet—
Therefore the Lord will smite with a scab the crown of
the head of the daughters of Zion,
And the Lord will lay bare their secret parts.

. . . .

And it shall come to pass
That instead of perfume there shall be rottenness

[27]3:9; 12–15.

And instead of a girdle a rope;
And instead of well-set hair baldness
And instead of a stately robe, a wrapping of sackcloth,
Branding instead of beauty.
Thy men shall fall by the sword,
Thy mighty men in battle.
And her gates shall lament and mourn
And she shall be despoiled and sit upon the ground.[28]

One of Isaiah's finest exhibitions not only of moral passion but of literary skill is embodied in his "Song of the Vineyard."[29] We do not know when he gave expression to it; the theme of the song occupied his mind throughout his life.

In the guise of a minstrel, Isaiah appeared in some public place and recited a vintage song, narrating the unfortunate experience of a friend. Perhaps it was on the occasion of a harvest festival, when the city of Jerusalem was crowded with peasants. A crowd must have gathered about him and listened with delight to the popular ballad:

Let me sing of my well-beloved a song
Of my beloved touching his vineyard.
My well-beloved had a vineyard
In a very fruitful hill;
And he made a trench about it,
    and gathered out the stones thereof,
And planted it with the choicest vine,
And built a tower in the midst of it,
And also hewed out a wine vat therein;
And he looked that it should bring forth grapes,
And it brought forth wild grapes.

And now, O inhabitants of Jerusalem,

283:16–17; 24–26.   295.

And men of Judah,
Judge, I pray you, between me and my vineyard.
What more could have been done for my vineyard,
That I have not done for it?
Wherefore, when I looked for it to yield grapes,
Did it yield wild grapes?
And now, let me tell you, I pray,
What I will do to my vineyard:
I will take away the hedge thereof,
And it shall be eaten up;
And I will break down the fence thereof,
And it shall be trodden down;
And I will lay it waste;
It shall not be pruned nor hoed.
But there shall come up briers and thorns.
I will also command the clouds
That they rain no rain upon it.

For the vineyard of the Lord of hosts
    is the house of Israel,
And the men of Judah His pleasant plant:
And He looked for justice, but behold oppression;
For righteousness, but behold a cry.[30]

The "wild grapes" of Judah are a debased aristocracy, avarice, sensuality, monopoly, dissipation, moral blindness, defiant unbelief. A series of "Woes" falls in rapid, stinging succession. His final point is:

Therefore as the tongue of fire devoureth the stubble,
And as the dry grass sinketh down in the flame,
So their root shall be of rottenness,
And their blossom shall go up as dust;
Because they have rejected the law of the Lord of Hosts,
And despised the word of the Holy One of Israel.[31]

[30] 5:1-7.   [31] 5:24.

God Himself will arise to judge His people; His hand
is outstretched in punishment. Revolution and anarchy
must inevitably follow the course the nation was pur-
suing.[32] Like Amos before him, Isaiah made the "Day of
the Lord" a day of judgment.

Like all his inspired colleagues, as critic of the social
order Isaiah was guided not by any one political philosophy nor by any principles in economics. He spoke not
as economist or social reformer. One force motivated him
and one ideal possessed him: the will of the Holy One
must prevail in the affairs of man.

"AND IT SHALL COME TO PASS AT THE END OF DAYS"

Speaking as the prophets did in hours of grave crises,
they were possessed by the belief that they were standing
at the brink of universal chaos. The "Day of the Lord"
would come, inevitably, and it would be a day of divine
wrath.

> Then the haughtiness of man shall be humbled;
> And the pride of man shall be brought low.
> The Lord alone shall be exalted on that day.[33]

But if the earth creaked, "as a cart creaketh that is
full of sheaves," and if the social order was "sinking like
dry grass in the fire," God lived. Beyond all the tumult
and the confusion, the injustice and the inhumanity was
the haunting presence of God. Purged of its vices, at
least a small remnant of the nation would arise purified,
ennobled, exalted, reconsecrated to the Holy One of Israel.
This belief it was that saved the prophets from despair
and made them dream heroic dreams.

[32]Read 9:8–10:4, plus 5:25–30.   [33]2:17.

Isaiah has endowed us with the tantalizing vision of a world lapped in justice and mercy, enjoying universal peace. Out of the chaos and cruelty of the world, out of his own fears and frustrations, out of his burning passion for the just and the holy were his dreams born; out of their own pains and passions have the sensitive and suffering men and women since the days of Isaiah been captivated and cheered by his vision.

A just, merciful, lovely world was in the womb of time, "and it shall come to pass in the end of days." Not a wildly conceived eschatological order but a Utopia—the Golden City—was Isaiah's dream. Unlike Hosea, and unlike the Greek poets, Isaiah dreamed of a Golden Age in the days to come, not seeing it in the days that were. Towards it mankind is moving, slowly, haltingly, but surely:

> And it shall come to pass in the end of days,
> That the mountain of the Lord's house shall
>   be established
> At the head of the mountains,
> And shall be exalted above the hills;
> And all the nations shall stream unto it.
>
> And many peoples shall go and say:
> "Come ye, and let us go up to the
>   mountain of the Lord
> To the house of the God of Jacob;
> That He may teach us of His ways
> And that we may walk in His paths;
> For out of Zion shall go forth instruction,
> And the word of the Lord from Jerusalem.

And He will judge between the nations
And will arbitrate for many peoples
And they will beat their swords into plowshares
And their spears into pruning-hooks.
Nation shall not lift up sword against nation,
Neither shall they learn war any more.

O house of Jacob, come ye and let us walk
In the light of the Lord.[34]

Upon the throne of Judah will be a scion of the house of Jesse. The stock that produced King David is not exhausted. The earthly and the divine will harmonize in him and produce a just ruler—the Hebrew counterpart to the philosopher-ruler:

And his name shall be Wonderful Counsellor,
God-like hero, Father forever, Prince of Peace.[35]

And the spirit of the Lord shall rest upon him,
The spirit of wisdom and understanding,
The spirit of counsel and might,
The spirit of knowledge and the fear of the Lord.
And his delight shall be in the fear of the Lord.
He shall not judge after the sight of his eyes,
Neither decide after the hearing of the ears;
But with righteousness shall he judge the poor,
And decide with equity for the meek of the earth;
And he shall smite the ruthless with the rod of his mouth
And with the breath of his lips shall he slay the wicked.
And righteousness shall be the girdle of his loins,
And faithfulness the girdle of his reins.[36]

Enraptured with his vision, the prophet dreams of the restoration of the age of innocence when even the preda-

[34] 2:2-5. The same passage occurs also in Micah 4:1-4.
[35] 9:5 (6).   [36] 11:2-5.

tory world will be conquered by the loving-kindness of God. The lion and the lamb, the leopard and the kid shall lie down together; the cow and the bear shall graze together, "and a little child shall lead them."

> They shall not hurt nor destroy
> On all My holy mountain;
> For the earth shall be full of
>   the knowledge of the Lord
> As the water covers the sea.[37]

Crushed to earth by the booted warriors, the gangster-statesmen and the crass manipulators in the sanctuaries of mankind, the vision rises reborn. In the hearts of his disciples the prophet's dream is sealed; "and it shall come to pass at the end of days."

[37] 11:9.

VII

MICAH

It hath been told thee, O man, what is good,
And what the Lord doth require of thee:
Only to do justly, and to love mercy,
And to walk humbly with thy God.

MICAH 6:8.

MICAH THE MORASTHITE

ISAIAH's ringing voice found a haunting echo in the utterances of Micah. In characteristically prophetic temper, this contemporary of Isaiah swells the chorus of Hebrew prophecy by arraying himself against the world and its vested corruption as the articulate conscience of his people:

> But I truly am full of power by the spirit of the Lord,
> And of justice and of might,
> To declare unto Jacob his transgression,
> And to Israel his sin.[1]

We have no information as to the relationship between Isaiah and Micah. That they were of like spirit is clear. But had they ever met? Had they ever exchanged views? Had they grieved together over the state of their people and dreamed together of a happier day? There is considerable evidence that Micah was influenced by Isaiah's

[1] 3:8.

77

words, probably after they had been reduced to writing.
Not only is there similarity of view but also of expression.[2]

Of Micah's personal life we know only his name, his
nativity, and the approximate date.[3] We must rely entirely on the content and the spirit of his utterances for
a glimpse of his personality.

He was a native of Moresheth, a small town, or perhaps
only a settlement, in the lowlands between the hills of
Judea and the coast of Philistia. He was a man of the
country, distinguished by the qualities of the man who
lives close to the soil, and close to the rooted peasantry.
The lowlands that held his village are "sufficiently de-
tached from the capital and the body of the land to
beget in her sons an independence of mind and feeling,
but so much upon the edge of the open world as to
endue them at the same time with that sense of the re-
sponsibilities of warfare, which the national statesmen,
aloof and at ease in Zion, could not possibly have shared."[4]

Micah had the peasant's suspicion of the city, his
strong, natural prejudice against luxury, self-indulgence,
and vices of the city. "He was pre-eminently the prophet
of the poor. . . . Knowing his fellow countrymen inti-
mately, and sympathizing profoundly with their sufferings and their wrongs, his spirit burned with indignation
as he beheld the injustice and tyranny of their rich op-

[2]See Cheyne, *CB,* Micah, p. 12.
[3]Scholars are in disagreement as to the exact date. One view is that
Micah spoke before the destruction of Samaria, which took place in
722–721 B.C., another view advanced by competent scholars is that his
activity as prophet fell between the years 705–701 B.C. See J. M. Powis
Smith, in *ICC* to Micah, p. 19. For a more conservative view, see Max
L. Margolis, *Micah,* Introduction.
[4]George Adam Smith, quoted *ICC* to Micah, p. 18.

pressors."[5] Fearless, merciless, severe, he denounced with
the unflinching justice of Amos and, nevertheless, pleaded
with the deep compassion of Hosea. How the call came to
him we do not know; he gives us no inaugural vision as
does Isaiah or Jeremiah, nor does he refer to his driving
force as champion of God; but it is evident that the cry
of the poor woke prophecy in his soul.

"THE HIRE OF A HARLOT"

Hear, ye peoples, all of you;
Hearken, O earth, and all that therein is;
And let the Lord God be witness against you,
The Lord from His holy temple.
For, behold, the Lord cometh forth out of His place,
And will come down, and tread upon the high places of
    the earth.
And the mountains shall be molten under Him,
And the valleys shall be cleft,
As wax before the fire,
As waters that are poured down a steep place.[6]

Thus, in words reminiscent of Isaiah, Micah summons
the nation before the divine tribunal. A corrupt religion
must lead to a disrupted social order. Samaria, central
shrine of northern Israel, and Jerusalem, the Holy City
of Judah, are nests of evil. The sanctuaries of God are
supported by the hire of harlots!

Avarice and arrogance are the driving passions of the
rich exploiters; they know no restraint. They covet fields
and seize them; they covet houses and take them away.
Thus they strip the poor man naked. And in this they
are abetted and blessed by a greedy clergy:

[5] J. M. Powis Smith, Micah, *ICC*, p. 18.   [6] 1:2-4.

Hear, I pray you, ye heads of Jacob,
And rulers of the house of Israel:
Is it not for you to know justice?
Who hate the good and love the evil;
Who rob their skin from off them,
And their flesh from off their bones—

. . . .

Who build Zion with blood,
And Jerusalem with iniquity.
The heads thereof judge for reward
And the priests thereof teach for hire,
And the prophets thereof divine for money.[7]

Prince, priest, and prophet are jointly responsible for the collapse of the nation. Micah announces the impending doom and chants a dirge over the nation. The devastation wrought by the Assyrian invader is revealed in his words.

"THE LORD IS A LIGHT UNTO ME"

Micah's message is not exhausted in denunciation. Denounce he does, with all the fire of an impassioned spirit; but he can also plead and pray for his people and hope that the evil may be averted. The purged remnant of the nation will yet affirm:

But as for me, I will look unto the Lord:
I will wait for the God of my salvation;
My God will hear me.
Rejoice not against me, O mine enemy:
Though I have fallen, I shall arise;
Though I sit in darkness, the Lord is a light unto me.[8]

[7]3:1-2; 10.

[8]7:7-8. Scholars are in radical disagreement as to how much of the book of Micah was spoken by the prophet Micah. One group of scholars confine Micah's authorship to the first three chapters of the book. See J. M. Powis Smith, *ICC*, Introduction. For the more traditional view, see Max L. Margolis, *Micah*, Introduction.

"WHEREWITH SHALL I COME BEFORE THE LORD?"

In the book of Micah the prophetic view of religion finds its most exalted expression. Whether it was said by Micah or by some one else whose words are embodied in the book of Micah is of no practical significance. The fact is that here we have the truest expression as to what constitutes true religion. It is one of the noblest passages in the Bible. It brings to a brilliant climax the teaching of the Bible on the relationship between God and man.

Addressing himself not to a fellow-national but to man —man the human being—the prophet raises a profound question and gives an answer that has become classic in Judaism and Christianity alike:

"Wherewith shall I come before the Lord,
And bow myself before God on high?
Shall I come before Him with burnt-offerings,
With calves of a year old?
Will the Lord be pleased with thousands of rams,
With ten thousands of rivers of oil?
Shall I give my first-born for my transgression,
The fruit of my body for the sin of my soul?"
It hath been told thee, O man, what is good,
And what the Lord doth require of thee:
Only to do justly, and to love mercy, and to walk humbly
    with thy God.[9]

With these words we take leave of Micah and of the eighth century B.C.

[9] 6:6–8.

VIII

THE BOILING CAULDRON

JUDAH's head was in the mouth of the Assyrian lion for about one hundred and thirty years. King Ahaz, acting contrary to the advice of Isaiah in the year 735 B.C., opened the door of Judah to a cat which soon gave birth to a tiger. Assyria came to Palestine to stay, to dominate, and to plunder. King Hezekiah was helpless under Assyrian domination; his successor, Manasseh, was an Assyrian puppet. Coming to the throne of Judah at the age of twelve, he reigned fifty-five years, and for fifty-five years he paid the Assyrian tribute, even threw his meager army into the field fighting Assyrian battles. Assyria grew to its largest proportions at this time. Her domain extended as far as Thebes, Egypt, and the Persian Gulf in the South, the Caucasus Mountains and the Caspian Sea in the North, deep into the Zagros Mountains in the East, and the Mediterranean coast in the West. Esarhaddon and his son and successor to the throne, Ashurbanipal, stretched her frontiers in every direction. In 633–632 B.C. Assyria invaded Egypt, her eternal enemy, and sacked Thebes. But these two emperors were the last in the victorious procession. Isaiah's prophecies, heralding the destruction of Assyria, were about to find fulfilment.

Assyria had been too successful. She died of "glorious

victories." Her constant warfare with Egypt had exhausted her. Other complications developed which sapped her strength. The fires of rebellion swept the far-flung empire. Two strong campaigns were needed to subdue Elam. Revolts flared up in Sidon, Tyre, Babylon, Arabia, Edom, Moab, Haurai, and upper Phœnicia. A civil war lasting seven years disrupted the empire from within. For some twelve years Assyria fought desperately beating the fires of revolt.

Meanwhile, the Babylonians and the Medes rose to power, and they were next door to weakened Assyria. They became the new terror of the North. Assyria was like a blind and shorn Samson. Her territories were falling away from her to these greedy powers. In vain did Egypt swallow her hatred of Assyria and throw an army in the field against Babylon. The final blow came in 612 B.C. when Nineveh, the capital of Assyria, fell before the Babylonian legions led by that remarkable warrior Nebuchadrezzar.[1] That was the beginning of the end. The mighty Assyrian empire soon collapsed completely, never to rise again. "Two hundred years later," writes one scholar,[2] "when Xenophon led his band of Greek adventurers past the site of Nineveh, he found no recollection of the name of the former mistress of the world."

REACTION IN JUDAH

Meanwhile, Judah was like a terrorized lamb. The tiny state—"the city of Judah," as Esarhaddon called her—

[1]For a characterization of Nebuchadrezzar, see J. F. McCurdy, *History, Prophecy and the Monuments* (N. Y., 1901), III, pp. 143 ff. An imaginative and spirited biography is G. R. Tabouis, *Nebuchadrezzar* (N. Y., 1931).

[2]J. M. Powis Smith, *ICC* to Zephaniah, p. 165.

was swept not only by Assyrian and Egyptian armies but by foreign gods and cults. Strong winds of nature-worship, blowing from the North, seduced her. Alliance with Assyria meant acceptance of Assyrian-Babylonian religious practices. Under King Manasseh, Judah relapsed into all the cults of Assyria and the Canaanitish peoples. The "hosts of heaven" returned and lured the masses. The inhabitants of the plains of Shinar were enamored of the stars. Sun worship returned; Ishtar, queen of heaven, was reinstated. Every house-top became an altar, Jeremiah complains:

> Seest thou not what they do in the cities of Judah and in the streets of Jerusalem? The children gather wood, and the fathers kindle the fire, and the women knead the dough, to make cakes to the queen of heaven, and to pour out drink-offerings unto other gods, that they may provoke Me.
>
> For according to the number of thy cities are thy gods, O Judah; and according to the number of the streets of Jerusalem have ye set up altars to the shameful thing, even altars to offer unto Baal. Therefore pray not thou for this people, neither lift up cry nor prayer for them; for I will not hear them in the time that they cry unto Me for their trouble.[3]

Back trooped the ghosts of the gods and goddesses. By imperial command and by an aroused passion they came; but they came, also, in response to the desperate plight of the masses. The Assyrian boot was heavy upon the neck of Judah. The land was improverished; tension, fear, and despair must have run their full course in the life of the unhappy masses and their leaders—or "misleaders"

[3] Jer. 7:17–18; 11:13.

as Isaiah called them. The people instinctively turned to the elemental forces of nature-worship.

Manasseh led the way. He sacrificed his own son. The biblical historian reports indignantly:

And he did that which was evil in the sight of the Lord, after the abominations of the nations, whom the Lord cast out before the children of Israel. For he built again the high places which Hezekiah his father had destroyed; and he reared up altars for Baal and made an Asherah, as did Ahab king of Israel, and worshipped all the host of heaven, and served them. And he built altars in the house of the Lord, whereof the Lord said: "In Jerusalem will I put My name." And he built altars for all the host of heaven in the two courts of the house of the Lord. And he made his son to pass through the fire, and practised soothsaying, and used enchantments, and appointed them that divined by a ghost or a familiar spirit: he wrought much evil in the sight of the Lord, to provoke Him.[4]

It must be remembered that these practices were not merely colorful pageantry; nature-worship meant a degrading morality. But this we have already considered.[5]

The prophetic voices were drowned in the rhythm of the sacred dance, in the incantations of wizards and enchanters and the chantings of priests and prophets of Baal. But the prophetic conscience was not deadened; driven under cover, it nevertheless challenged, protested, and rebelled.

"Manasseh shed innocent blood very much," the biblical scribe continues his sad chronicle. The reference is

[4]II Kings 21:2–6.   [5]See Chap. III.

not quite clear. Who were these victims whose blood was shed and why? The reference, it seems, is to the persecution of the prophets. The disciples of Amos, Hosea, Isaiah, and Micah must have drawn the wrath of the idolatrous king and his subordinates. It is the belief of scholars that much of the preachments of the eighth-century prophets were reduced to writing in reaction to the persecution in the days of Manasseh (692–638 B.C.). The editions made at that time became the nuclei of the editions now before us.

Manasseh reigned fifty-four years; his son and successor, Amon, was on the throne only one year when he was assassinated. The latter's son, Josiah, was a child of eight when he became the King of Judah. The boy-king came under the influence of the persecuted prophetic group. Just how we do not know; but his mind and conscience were trained by the "small remnant" in whose hearts were sealed the oracles as expounded by the prophets. Upon reaching maturity and independence of action, Josiah instituted a sweeping reform of the religious, economic, and social life of Judah. It is known as the Reformation of Josiah. Its controlling principles are embodied in the book of Deuteronomy.

A PROPHETIC LAW BOOK

Free and untrammeled as the prophets were in proclaiming the word of God, their pronouncements were not left to vibrate and fade out in the rarefied atmosphere of inspired speech. Their divine wrath geared the machinery of government. The book of laws holding their spirit and specific teachings is Deuteronomy. The core of the book as we have it today was proclaimed by King Josiah in the year 621 B.C.

The immediate legislative reforms enacted by Josiah were two: the centralization of worship and the establishment of an authoritative priesthood. The local shrines that dotted Judah were outlawed. They were nests of local idolatries of all sorts: Canaanitish nature-worship flourished at these wayside shrines, secluded groves, holy wells, springs, trees, and mountain tops. No effective reform could be executed as long as these shrines functioned. Attached to these sacred places were idolatrous priests. The Reformation of Josiah abolished the local shrines and outlawed the priests. Many of them were slaughtered. It centralized all worship at the national shrine on Mt. Zion, and placed in charge the Levites as the only duly accredited priests.

Seeking to make their reforms authoritative and effective, the authors report it as having been decreed by Moses in the steppes of Moab on the way to the Promised Land. It is Israel's supreme legislator who is the author of the code, and he received it at Mt. Sinai, directly from God. Thus the laws and the spirit in which they are to be obeyed are of supreme authority. Present-day scholarship, however, sees in Deuteronomy a revision—at many points a radical revision and even annulment—of earlier laws.[6]

[6]For a detailed and authoritative analysis of Deuteronomy, see S. R. Driver *ICC, Deuteronomy,* Introduction; or George Adam Smith, *CB, Deuteronomy,* Introduction. For a challenge of this point of view, see Joseph Reider, *Deuteronomy,* Introduction (Phila., 1937).

THE FUNDAMENTAL PRINCIPLE

The fundamental principle controlling the exhortation and the specific legislation of Deuteronomy is in the interpretation of God, Israel, and the covenant between God and Israel.

God is One and unique. He is "the God of gods and the Lord of lords." His rule is supreme, just, and merciful. Israel's battle-cry is sounded here for the first time; this affirmation has bound the ages of Israel, consecrated the Jew as the religious idealist among the nations and nerved him against all the furies of history: "Hear, O Israel: the Lord is our God, the Lord is One."[7] All other gods are false and must not be tolerated. "Thou shalt have no other gods before me." Spiritual, no image may be made of Him.

Called of God, Israel is a holy people, "His peculiar possession." Out of love and faithfulness to His word, as spoken to the progenitor of the race, He called Israel to be His prophet in the world, redeemed him from Egypt, led him through the wilderness "as on eagle's wings," and brought him to the Promised Land.

For thou art a holy people unto the Lord thy God: the Lord thy God hath chosen thee to be His own treasure, out of all the peoples that are upon the face of the earth. The Lord did not set His love upon you, nor choose you, because ye were more in number than any people—for ye were the fewest of all peoples—but because the Lord loved you, and because He would keep the oath which He swore unto your fathers, hath the Lord brought you out with a mighty hand, and redeemed you out of the house

7 6:4.

of bondage, from the hand of Pharaoh king of Egypt.
Know therefore that the Lord thy God, He is God; the
faithful God, who keepeth covenant and mercy with them
that love Him and keep His commandments to a thousand generations; and repayeth them that hate Him to
their face, to destroy them; he will not be slack to him
that hateth Him, He will repay him to his face. Thou
shalt therefore keep the commandment, and the statutes,
and the ordinances, which I command thee this day, to
do them.[8]

Israel must fear Him and love Him. The declaration
of God's unity is followed with the command: "And thou
shalt love the Lord thy God with all thy heart, with all
thy soul, and with all thy might." If Israel is set apart
from the nations of the world, it is that the priest-people
must not be defiled by the idolatries of the world. Fidelity
to his priestly vows will bring the blessings of God; in-
fidelity will bring His curses.

Thus a covenant exists between God and Israel. Love
and duty seal this covenant. Every soul in Israel, from
those ragged hordes who stood at Sinai through the ages
yet unborn, personally participated in the making and
in the execution of this covenant.

Ye are standing this day all of you before the Lord
your God: your heads, your tribes, your elders, and your
officers, even all the men of Israel, your little ones, your
wives, and thy stranger that is in the midst of thy camp,
from the hewer of thy wood unto the drawer of thy water;
that thou shouldst enter into the covenant of the Lord
thy God—and into His oath—which the Lord thy God
maketh with thee this day; that He may establish thee this
day unto Himself for a people, and that He may be unto

[8]Deut. 7:6-11.

thee a God, as He spoke unto thee, and as He swore unto thy fathers, to Abraham, to Isaac, and to Jacob. Neither with you only do I make this covenant and this oath; but with him that standeth here with us this day before the Lord our God, and also with him that is not here with us this day.[9]

PROPHETIC PRINCIPLES

A prophetic law book, Deuteronomy harmonizes the spirit of the prophet with the method of the legislator. Civil statutes and ceremonial rites become vehicles of great moral principles. The close relationship between the provisions of Deuteronomy and Hebrew prophecy may be seen in clear form at several points.

The conception of God, Israel's mission, the meaning of holiness, the emphasis on ethics and morality, are prophetic; they are the motivations of Deuteronomic legislation.

God is a moral power, Who requires that His will be done. What He requires of man is social justice, personal integrity, mercy, love, and duty. Micah's superb formula —"It hath been told thee, O man, what is good and what the Lord doth require of thee: Only to do justly and love mercy and walk humbly with thy God"—might have been the Deuteronomist's motto.

God is supreme. He alone reigns. And He is just.

Know this day, and lay it to thy heart, that the Lord, He is God in heaven above and upon the earth beneath; there is none else.[10]

Holiness is in terms of morality and ethics. Isaiah especially had interpreted holiness in this sense. Love of

[9]Deut. 29:9–14 (10–15).   [10]Deut. 4:39.

God means love of neighbor. Hence the emphasis in Deuteronomy is upon a just man in a just world. This is to be realized not by virtue of any economic formula or political platform, but by obeying God. This, as we have seen, is characteristic of the prophets as social reformers.

Deuteronomy thus stresses justice between man and man: "Justice, justice shalt thou pursue." It demands honest judges and just judgment, just weights and measures.

Thou shalt not have in thy bag diverse weights, a great and a small. Thou shalt not have in thy house diverse measures, a great and a small. A perfect and just weight shalt thou have; a perfect and just measure shalt thou have; that thy days may be long upon the land which the Lord thy God giveth thee. For all that do such things, even all that do unrighteously, are an abomination unto the Lord thy God.[11]

Special security is sought for the underdog: the indigent, the slave, the bankrupt, the alien, the landless, the war captive, the widow, the orphan, the criminal persecuted by the avenger, the Levite lacking in worldly goods, the abused wife; mercy is extended even to the animals. The memory of Egyptian bondage is turned into an ethical motivation: "Thou shalt remember that thou wast a bondman in Egypt, and the Lord thy God redeemed thee thence; therefore, I command thee to do this thing."[12]

Like Hosea a century earlier, the Deuteronomist attributes the national catastrophes to the violation of the word of God. Like Hosea, the prophet-legislator repudi-

[11]Deut. 25:13–16.   [12]Deut. 24:18.

ates Canaanitish nature-worship. God, not Baal, it is that
wakes the earth with sunshine and rain and stimulates it
to yield its bounties. Like Hosea, further, he emphasizes
God's love for Israel and exhorts Israel to the loving
service of his God. The warmth of emotion and the tender
compassion so characteristic of Hosea permeate Deuteronomy.

Such close similarity is there between Deuteronomy and
Jeremiah that for a time scholars believed that Jeremiah
had a hand in writing it. A long list of whole clauses and
phrases appearing in both has been compiled.[13]

But the Deuteronomist was a legislator as well as a
prophet. He therefore diverges from the prophetic at
several points. He has much more respect for ritual and
ceremonial; he shows a larger sympathy for the priest;
he is much more particularistic in his conception of the
nation. His practical turn of mind and the pressure of
a heathenism openly cultivated a generation earlier are the
major explanations of this.

Deuteronomy is practical prophecy. The word of God
is made the rule of life for the individual and for the
nation.

DEATH OF "GOOD KING JOSIAH"

Josiah did not live long enough to drive his reforms
deep into the life of Judah. Pharaoh Necho, marching
northward to aid hard-pressed Assyria, Egypt's historic
enemy, trapped King Josiah and slew him. The death of
Josiah was a hard blow to Judah. He was an enlightened
monarch who had brought a new moral content into the

[13]S. R. Driver, *ICC, Deuteronomy*, p. xcii.

life of the nation. His reign represents one of the noblest periods in Hebrew history.

Josiah's younger son, Jehoahaz, came to the throne by the will of the people. Necho deposed and imprisoned him, and placed upon the throne his own choice, Josiah's older son, Jehoiakim, who was more pliable in the hands of the Egyptian. Jehoiakim was unworthy to succeed his father. He was a greedy puppet, imposing ruinous taxation to enrich his Egyptian master. The reforms his father had instituted were quickly reversed. Judah was once again in a period of reaction.[14]

SCYTHIANS

Meantime, a horde of barbarians known as Scythians poured out of Europe across the Caucasus into Asia Minor and Palestine, terrorizing the world about them. They were wandering bands of Indo-European stock, huge of build, famous for their cruelty and savagery. They were of little skill against fortified cities, however; that is what saved many a city in their path. They swept down the coastal plain of Judah, plundering unfortified cities, pushing southward toward the Nile delta. The prophets Zephaniah and Jeremiah saw God's judgment of the nation in this new invasion. We shall read subsequently from Jeremiah on this point. Here let us heed to Zephaniah, Nahum, and Habakkuk.

ZEPHANIAH

A great-great-grandson of Hezekiah, Zephaniah was a prophet of royal descent. He knew at close range the life

[14]II Kings 23:29–24:7.

of Jerusalem and the Temple, and was violently critical
of the upper classes. He may have been one of the prophets
who supported the Reformation of Josiah. He was probably in the early twenties when that revolution was in-
stigated in 621 B.C.

The little book that holds his utterances begins with a
dismal, black picture of the moral life about him. The
prophet is grieved at what is transpiring and horrified
at what is to befall the nation and the world. "The great
day of the Lord," is at hand; war and famine will sweep
the earth. Destruction, plague, and exile will annihilate
the nation.

His indictment of Judah, and of the larger humanity
as well, is reminiscent of the austere accents of Amos.
Judah is "a shameless nation"; Jerusalem is rebellious,
faithless, polluted with every idolatry. Every group within her is corrupt; her princes are robbers, her judges are
greedy, her priests are idolatrous, her prophets are false.
Moloch is worshipped, not God. In God who presides
over the destinies of men and nations there is boastful
disbelief: "The Lord will not do good, neither will He do
evil."

Therefore the Day of the Lord will come, and His judgments will fall mercilessly. Zephaniah's mind must have
been incited by the Scythian hordes sweeping down
Palestine:

> Near at hand is the great day of the Lord;
> Near and speeding fast!
> Near at hand is the bitter day of the Lord.
> Then the warrior will cry in terror!
> A day of wrath is that day;

A day of trouble and distress,
A day of desolation and waste,
A day of darkness and gloom.
A day of cloud and thundercloud;
A day of the trumpet and battle-cry,
Against the fortified cities,
And against the lofty battlements.[15]

Not on Judah alone will the judgments of God fall; the larger world as well will know His wrath.

But God is not a wanton fury wrecking His world. He seeks to cleanse, to refine, and to save, if mankind would only co-operate with Him:

Seek ye the Lord, all ye humble of the earth,
That have executed His ordinances;
Seek righteousness, seek humility.
It may be ye shall be hid in the day
    of the Lord's anger.[16]

Zephaniah echoes his predecessors in the prophetic procession. A remnant will be saved. Purged, humanity will arise reborn, redeemed of its evil. Then the nations will speak a purer language; Israel, "an afflicted and poor people . . . shall take refuge in the name of the Lord."

The remnant of Israel shall not do iniquity,
Nor speak lies,
Neither shall a deceitful tongue be found in their mouth;
For they shall feed and lie down,
And none shall make them afraid.[17]

Zephaniah's prophecies, rising from black depths of despair, swell like a mighty chorus in a pæan of joy—the joy of God in the hearts of the humble:

[15]1:14–18.　　　[16]2:3.　　　[17]3:13.

Sing, O daughter of Zion,
Shout, O Israel;
Be glad and rejoice with all thy heart,
O daughter of Jerusalem.
The Lord hath taken away thy judgments,
He hath cast out thine enemy;
The King of Israel, even the Lord,
    is in the midst of thee;
Thou shalt not fear evil any more.
In that day it shall be said to Jerusalem:
"Fear thou not;
O Zion, let not thy hands be slack.
The Lord thy God is in the midst of thee,
A Mighty One who will save;
He will rejoice over thee with joy,
He will be silent in His love,
He will joy over thee with singing."[18]

NAHUM

The bitter hatred of the Judæan masses against the Assyrian invader is voiced in the prophecies of Nahum. A terrible beauty permeates the little book. A jealous and avenging God has unleashed his fury against a prostitute nation.

We know nothing at all of Nahum's life. All the biographic material we are given is the phrase, "Nahum the Elkoshite." Elkosh has not been identified.

From the contents and spirit of the prophecies it is quite evident that Nahum spoke shortly before the fall of Nineveh in 612 B.C. He points to the fall of Thebes and anticipates with glee a similar fate for Nineveh.

Unlike his prophetic colleagues, Nahum has no ethical

[18]3:14–17.

message for his people. He speaks no reproof and enun-
ciates no moral ideal. Not words of faith but a cry for
vengeance falls from his inspired lips. He gives brilliant
expression to a bitter hatred for the Assyrian lion that
devastated Judah.

> Keep thy feasts, O Judah,
> Perform thy vows;
> For the wicked one shall no more pass through thee;
> He is utterly cut off.[19]

Doom hangs over Nineveh. In one of the most brilliant
bits of descriptive writing in the Bible, Nahum pictures
the assailing cavalry:

> Woe to the bloody city!
> It is all full of lies and rapine;
> The prey departeth not.
> Hark! the whip, and hark!
>   the rattling of wheels;
> And prancing horses, and
>   bounding chariots;
> The horsemen charging,
> And the flashing sword,
>   and the glittering spear;
> And a multitude of slain,
>   and a heap of carcasses;
> And there is no end of the corpses,
> And they stumble upon their corpses;
> Because of the multitude of the harlotries
>   of the well-favoured harlot.
> The mistress of witchcrafts,
> That selleth nations through her harlotries,
> And families through her witchcrafts.
> Behold, I am against thee, saith the Lord of hosts,

[19]2:1 (1:15).

And I will uncover thy skirts upon thy face,
And I will show the nations thy nakedness,
And the kingdoms thy shame.
And I will cast detestable things upon thee,
    and make thee vile,
And will make thee as dung.
And it shall come to pass, that all
    they that look upon thee
Shall flee from thee,
And say: "Nineveh is laid waste;
Who will bemoan her?
Whence shall I seek comforters for thee?"[20]

Great will be the rejoicing among the nations:

All that hear the report of thee
Clap their hands over thee;
For upon whom hath not thy wickedness
    passed continually?[21]

HABAKKUK

The name Habakkuk may mean "ardent embrace."
Saint Jerome, writing in the fourth century, so explains
Habakkuk's name, on the basis of certain legends. "He
is called 'embrace' either because of his love to the Lord,
or because he wrestled with God." Habakkuk did both.
He loved God and wrestled with Him. Out of the per-
plexities that beset him, he emerged a prophet of faith.
"Thus saith the Lord" came to him not as a vision from
heaven, but out of his personal agony of heart and mind.
He struggled with God and *achieved* faith.

Beyond his name we know nothing of him. That he

[20]3:1–7.   [21]3:19.

prophesied between the years 608 and 597 B.C. is clear
from his utterances.

It was a noisy, cruel, and perplexing age, particularly
to a sensitive soul such as Habakkuk seems to have been.
Assyria had crumbled into chaos; Babylon was the new
terror in the north—"a bitter and impetuous nation";
Judah was on the brink of chaos; within Judah were
violence and injustice. If a just and merciful God pre-
sided over the destinies of men and nations, why this
cruelty and evil?

The prophet's inner struggle is presented in dramatic
form. To his anguished "Why?" God replies:

Look ye among the nations, and behold,
And wonder marvellously;
For, behold, a work shall be wrought in your days,
Which ye will not believe though it be told you.
For, lo, I raise up the Chaldeans,
That bitter and impetuous nation,
That march through the breadth of the earth,
To possess dwelling-places that are not theirs.
They are terrible and dreadful;
Their law and their majesty proceed from themselves.
Their horses also are swifter than leopards,
And are more fierce than the wolves of the desert;
And their horsemen spread themselves;
Yea, their horsemen come from far,
They fly as a vulture that hasteth to devour.
They come all of them for violence;
Their faces are set eagerly as the east wind;
And they gather captives as the sand.
And they scoff at kings,
And princes are a derision unto them;

They deride every stronghold,
For they heap up earth, and take it.
Then their spirit doth pass over and transgress,
And they become guilty:
Even they who impute their might unto their god.[22]

The visitation of God is on the way. Now it is Babylon that is "the rod of His anger." But the prophet's perplexities deepen. The Babylonians are outrageously cruel; they exult in their evil. Why does God, the Holy One, employ so cruel a weapon, and why does He look on in silence?

Thou that art of eyes too pure to behold evil,
And that canst not look on mischief,
Wherefore lookest Thou, when they deal treacherously,
And holdest Thy peace, when the wicked swalloweth up
The man that is more righteous than he?[23]

Like a watchman upon a tower, the man of God takes his position and waits for His answer. The answer comes:

And the Lord answered me, and said:
"Write the vision,
And make it plain upon tables,
That a man may read it swiftly.
For the vision is yet for the appointed time,
And it declareth of the end, and doth not lie;
Though it tarry, wait for it;
Because it will surely come, it will not delay."

.   .   .   .

But the righteous shall live by his faith.[24]

The Chaldean power must fall because of its inner

221:5–11.   231:13.   242:2–4.

rottenness. It will burst like a bubble; it will collapse like
a crooked wall.

The last words of the prophet mingle with the blood
and tears of Judah. It was a time when the righteous,
if they were to live at all, had to live by faith. The Babylonian was at the gates of Jerusalem. The prophet calls
down the woes of heaven upon him for his lust of conquest,
his rapacity, his oppression, his humiliation of fallen
kings and nations, and his stupid idolatries. But the Lord
is still in His holy Temple.

"Let all the earth keep silence before Him."

The last chapter of the book of Habakkuk is a superb
psalm, resembling the nature psalms of the Psalter in
grandeur of thought and beauty of expression. It was not
spoken nor written by Habakkuk. It is clearly of a later
age. Its indomitable faith, however, is a fitting epilogue
to Habakkuk, and a prologue to Jeremiah:

> For though the fig-tree shall not blossom,
> Neither shall fruit be in the vines;
> The labour of the olive shall fail,
> And the fields shall yield no food;
> The flock shall be cut off from the fold,
> And there shall be no herd in the stalls;
> Yet I will rejoice in the Lord,
> I will exult in the God of my salvation.[25]

[25] 3:17–18.

IX

JEREMIAH

If I say: "I will not make mention of Him,
Nor speak any more in His name,"
Then there is in my heart as it were a burning fire
Shut up in my bones,
And I weary myself to hold it in,
But cannot.

JEREMIAH 20:9.

THE WORLD OF JEREMIAH

JEREMIAH'S activity as prophet spanned a period of forty fearful years. Between the years 626 B.C. when the call to prophecy completely possessed him, and 586 B.C. when he disappeared from view, engulfed in the tragedy of Judah, he drained to the dregs the bitter cup God had put to his mouth. He has been called "the weeping prophet," "the man of sorrow." That he was. From his name is derived our word, "jeremiad." Frequently did he curse the day of his birth:

> Cursed be the day
> Wherein I was born;
> The day wherein my mother bore me,
> Let it not be blessed.
> Cursed be the man who brought tidings
> To my father, saying:
> "A man-child is born unto thee";
> Making him very glad.

102

> And let that man be as the cities
> Which the Lord overthrew,
>   and repented not;
> And let him hear a cry
>   in the morning,
> And an alarm at noontide;
> Because He slew me not
>   from the womb;
> And so my mother would have been
>   my grave,
> And her womb always great.
> Wherefore came I forth out of the womb
> To see labour and sorrow,
> That my days should be consumed in shame?[1]

But the truer meaning of his name is "appointed of the Lord" or "exalted of the Lord." Exalted he was, and exalting. He could thrill with the joy of God's presence as a violin in the hands of the master. Sensitive, responsive, deeply mystic, subject to rapidly shifting moods, haunted by visions, depressed by fears and buoyed by an unflinching faith, he had an enormous capacity for deep compassion, tender mercy, and pain of soul; he could also speak with an enraged eloquence, breathing the fierce fury of an avenging God.

Jeremiah's life was intertwined with the fate of Judah, which in turn was at the mercy of world forces, whirling like a weathercock in a storm. As we have already seen,[2] it was a time of shifting empires. Mighty Assyria, like a dazed giant, was on the defensive against two upstart powers, Babylon in the valley of the Euphrates, and Media in her mountain fastnesses farther north. Egypt was on the decline. From the banks of the Nile she might

[1] 20:14–18.   [2] See Chap. VIII.

have watched with abundant satisfaction Assyria tottering to her ruin, but she was fearful of the new powers shaking the North. Young, and more ambitious than wise, Pharaoh Necho hastening to the aid of Assyria— invading Judah and murdering Josiah on the way—was speeding to his own doom. At Carchemish—in northern Syria, commanding one of the principal fords of the Euphrates—in the year 605 B.C., the Egyptian army was routed. That was a decisive blow. Henceforth Babylon was the new fierce lion. All of the once mighty Assyria, Syria, and Palestine—from "the brook of Egypt unto the river Euphrates"—became Babylonian provinces. Nebuchadrezzar halted his pursuit of Pharaoh Necho at the very banks of the Nile, forced by his father's death. The young general had to hurry home to be crowned king of the mighty upstart power. The rise of Babylon-Media was the turning point of the age. It determined the destiny of Judah.

Meanwhile, Judah was in constant turmoil under the impact of these world-forces. Black, ominous clouds were gathering. Jeremiah heard the rumbling of thunder, and his heart ached for his land and people. Would the divine wrath finally break? Would God have mercy and avert the evil decree? Was Judah doomed? The unhappy prophet was convinced it was. He announced it as an accomplished fact. Nevertheless he hoped—hoped against hope. Pathetically, tenderly, he pleaded with Jerusalem to change its ways and live.

> O Jerusalem, wash thy heart from wickedness,
> That thou mayest be saved.[3]

[3] 4:14.

And again:

> As a cistern welleth with her waters,
> So she welleth with her wickedness;
> Violence and spoil is heard in her;
> Before Me continually is sickness and wounds.
>
> Be thou corrected, O Jerusalem,
> Lest My soul be alienated from thee,
> Lest I make thee desolate,
> A land not inhabited.[4]

The religious, economic reformation under Josiah, the assassination of this noble king, waves of marauders sweeping the land, unfortunate successions to the throne, heavy taxation under a puppet king, flirtations with Egypt, futile rebellions against Babylon, social-religious degeneracy—these kept Judah in ferment and confirmed Jeremiah in his conviction that the nation was on the brim of chaos.

A WORD AS TO THE TEXT

Jeremiah wrote down his prophecies from memory twenty-two years after he had begun speaking them. This manuscript was destroyed by King Jehoiakim, as we shall see. In defiance Jeremiah reproduced another document—again from memory—adding much to it in a fit of anger. Moreover, this second, enlarged edition passed from editor to editor for some three hundred and eighty years. The Hebrew edition of the utterances of Jeremiah as we have it today received its final form about the year 200 B.C. Jeremiah had disappeared from view as prophet in the year 586 B.C., when Judah collapsed before the onslaught of the Babylonian invader. Those were stormy

[4]6:7–8.

centuries. Judah experienced many severe crises; empires collapsed about her, and she was on the edge of doom again and again. The Babylonian Exile, the fall of Babylon, and the rise of Persia, the return to Palestine, the rebuilding of the Temple, much strife within, strong tension of conflicting loyalties, friction with neighboring peoples, the coming of Alexander the Great, the waves of Hellenism submerging Judah and the Temple, and the new emphases given by new generations of teachers—all these made it inevitable that pious students of the word of God as recorded by Jeremiah should unwittingly interpret them in the light of the new circumstances. Notations these students made in the margin of the manuscript were embodied in the text itself by later scribes. Thus much foreign material found its way into the prophetic books; some material must have been lost. While this is true of much of the Bible, it is especially true of the book of Jeremiah.

The book of Jeremiah, therefore, as it stands today in our Bible, like all the prophetic books, cannot be taken as a verbatim report of what the prophet actually spoke.[5] It is particularly difficult to establish Jeremiah's utterances as a young man. These come to us from the mouth of an old man, beaten, reviled, and tormented of soul.

YOUTH

Introspective and finely articulate, his personality and the facts of his life are more completely revealed than is

---

[5]For a brief and lucid exposition of the growth of the book of Jeremiah, the reader is referred to George Adam Smith, *Jeremiah* (1925), Lecture I, or to S. R. Driver, *The Book of the Prophet Jeremiah,* Introduction, (1906); for a more detailed study, he should turn to A. B. Davidson in Hastings, *Dictionary of the Bible.*

the case with any other prophet. The whole book of Jeremiah is the confession of a suffering soul. Unfortunately, the records are confused and blank pages are many.

He was the son of Hilkiah, "of the priests that were in Anathoth in the land of Benjamin." Anathoth was three miles northeast of Jerusalem. Perched high on the mountain ridge, it commanded a broad view of Ephraim and the Jordan valley to the north and Jerusalem to the south. To these views his mind reverted again and again, as if seeking consolation. The date of his birth is unknown, but it was toward the end of the long and evil reign of Manasseh (698–642 B.C.). Micah and Isaiah were in their unknown graves by this time. The aged in Judah, when Jeremiah was a little boy, may have remembered them.

Jeremiah must have been exposed to the culture of the priestly class. A deep religious spirit permeated him from childhood; but no trace of the pompous, presumptuous ecclesiastic can be detected in him. Early in his life he came into conflict with the priests of Anathoth. Once at least they plotted his assassination.

I was like a docile lamb that is led
    to the slaughter;
And I knew not that they had devised
    devices against me (saying):
"Let us destroy the tree with the fruit thereof,
And let us cut him off from the land of the living,
That his name may be no more remembered."[6]

He never married. Not for him were the normal joys of life. Living, as he was convinced he was, on the edge of

[6] 11:19.

doom, he had no moral right to bring children into a collapsing world.

The word of the Lord came also unto me, saying:
Thou shalt not take thee a wife,
Neither shalt thou have sons or daughters in this place.
For thus saith the Lord concerning the sons and concerning the daughters that are born in this place, and concerning their mothers that bore them, and concerning their fathers that begot them in this land:

They shall die of grievous deaths;
They shall not be lamented,
  neither shall they be buried,
They shall be as dung upon the face
  of the ground;
And they shall be consumed by the sword,
  and by famine;
And their carcasses shall be meat
  for the fowls of heaven,
And for the beasts of the earth.[7]

He seems to have been haunted by the happiness denied him. Frequently he repeats his conviction, with which he could not live in peace:

I will cause to cease from the cities of Judah and from the streets of Jerusalem the voice of mirth and the voice of gladness, the voice of the bridegroom and the voice of the bride: for the land shall become a waste.[8]

He moved in crowds, talked to mobs, wept and hoped, and was alone in the world—alone with his God.

[7]16:1–4.   [8]7:34; 16:9; 25:10; 33:11.

SCYTHIAN MENACE

The waves of Scythian barbarians spilling over the Caucasus Mountains, ravaging the coastal plain of Judah about the year 625 B.C., sent terror into the heart of Jeremiah and wrung from him his first prophetic words. The invasion was the first event in the lifetime of Jeremiah to have a telling effect upon him. Like his contemporary, Zephaniah, he saw in this invasion the punishment of God upon a sinful nation. His darkest fears were coming true. Like a scorching wind from the north these plundering hordes spread havoc:

Declare ye in Judah, and publish in Jerusalem,
And say: "Blow ye the horn in the land";
Cry aloud and say:
"Assemble yourselves, and let us go
    into the fortified cities."
Set up a standard toward Zion;
Put yourselves under covert, stay not;
For I will bring evil from the north,
And a great destruction.
A lion is gone up from his thicket,
And a destroyer of nations
Is set out, gone forth from his place;
To make thy land desolate,
That thy cities be laid waste,
    without inhabitant.

For this gird you with sackcloth,
Lament and wail;
For the fierce anger of the Lord
Is not turned back from us.
And it shall come to pass at that day,
Saith the Lord,

That the heart of the king shall fail,
And the heart of the princes;
And the priests shall be astonished,
And the prophets shall wonder.[9]

The frenzy of the marauder is in Jeremiah's description; "the sword reacheth unto the soul."

> Behold, he cometh up as clouds,
> And his chariots are as the whirlwind;
> His horses are swifter than eagles.
> Woe unto us! for we are undone.[10]

A picture of desolation flashes before the prophet's excited mind:

> I beheld the earth,
> And, lo, it was waste and void;
> And the heavens, and they had no light.
> I beheld the mountains, and, lo, they trembled,
> And all the hills moved to and fro.
> I beheld, and, lo, there was no man,
> And all the birds of the heavens were fled.
> I beheld, and, lo, the fruitful field
>   was a wilderness,
> And all the cities thereof were broken down
> At the presence of the Lord,
> And before His fierce anger.[11]

What this meant to a sensitive spirit, Jeremiah himself tells us in haunting syllables:

My bowels, my bowels! I writhe in pain!
The chambers of my heart!
My heart moaneth within me!
I cannot hold my peace!

[9] 4:5–9.   [10] 4:13.   [11] 4:23–26.

Because thou hast heard, O my soul,
    the sound of the horn,
The alarm of war.
Destruction followeth upon destruction,
For the whole land is spoiled;
Suddenly are my tents spoiled,
My curtains in a moment.
How long shall I see the standard,
Shall I hear the sound of the horn?[12]

The threat of the invasion dispelled Jeremiah's diffidence and compelled him to assume the role of prophet. But the tide of invasion shifted to other shores. Judah, it would seem, escaped.[13] Jeremiah's excited utterances labelled him as a panicky person. By the logic of the crowd he was a false and frenzied prophet.

DRAFTED

Jeremiah was drafted into the ranks of Hebrew prophecy. A power higher than himself seized him and enthralled him and pitched him against the world with the command to conquer or be conquered. Unlike Amos, who does not seem to have hesitated in presenting himself at Beth-el and hurling his invectives, unlike Isaiah, who, transported, leaped to his feet in the sanctuary with the eager cry, "Here am I; send me," Jeremiah was fearful

[12]4:19–21. The above quotations were inspired by the Scythian invasion. By the time they were committed to writing, some twenty years later, the Scythian scare had passed and a new menace was seen in the North in the person of Nebuchadrezzar. "My bowels, my bowels." The bowels were considered the seat of emotions; hence the expression is equivalent to our "My heart, my heart!"

[13]Scholars are not agreed on this point. See J. Skinner, *Prophecy and Religion*, Chap. III, and J. F. McCurdy, *History, Prophecy and the Monuments* (N. Y., 1901), II, pp. 395 ff.

to heed the voice within him. He accepted the call reluctantly; but, once he yielded, he prosecuted his commission with the abandon of holy zeal. This inner conflict, however, haunted him to the end.

He announces simply that he was predestined for his work as prophet of God, that he fought off his responsibility, that he finally was overpowered, and that he speaks as one ordained by the Supreme Master. And not to Israel alone is he to speak but to all the world. "A prophet unto the nations have I appointed thee." At once reluctant and eager, his is the voice of the Lord:

And the word of the Lord came unto me, saying:
Before I formed thee in the belly I knew thee,
And before thou camest forth out of the womb I sanctified
    thee;
I have appointed thee a prophet unto the nations.

Then said I: "Ah, Lord God! behold, I cannot speak;
    for I am a child." But the Lord said unto me:
Say not: I am a child;
For to whomsoever I shall send thee thou shalt go,
And whatsoever I shall command thee thou shalt speak.
Be not afraid of them;
For I am with thee to deliver thee,
Saith the Lord.

Then the Lord put forth His hand, and touched my
    mouth;
        and the Lord said unto me:

Behold, I have put My words in thy mouth;
See, I have this day set thee over the nations
        and over the kingdoms,

To root out and to pull down,
And to destroy and to overthrow;
To build, and to plant.[14]

Jeremiah was a man of conflict. Called to assume his duties as prophet, he protests pathetically: "Ah, Lord God, I cannot speak for I am only a child." But the Lord's hand was upon him. How was he to rebel? Passionate for peace, he was compelled to proclaim the certainty of war and see his land soaked with blood; ardently patriotic, he was called upon to counsel his nation to submit to the invader; deeply religious, he spent his life denouncing the established religion of his people as immoral and its priests as flunkies; convinced that a God of justice and loving-kindness directed the destinies of men and nations, he saw, like Job, brutal contradiction of it wherever he turned. Against priest and prophet, against ruler and ruled he had to take a stand and be indomitable as a wall of brass:

Thou therefore gird up thy loins, and arise, and speak unto them all that I command thee; be not dismayed at them, lest I dismay thee before them. For, behold, I have made thee this day a fortified city, and an iron pillar, and brazen walls, against the whole land, against the kings of Judah, against the princes thereof, against the priests thereof, and against the people of the land. And·they shall fight against thee; but they shall not prevail against thee; for I am with thee, saith the Lord, to deliver thee.[15]

Spiritual conflict is the main characteristic in the personality of Jeremiah.

[14]1:4–10.   [15]1:17–19.

Jeremiah raised his voice in prophetic utterance with a bitter indictment of his nation, condemning in scathing terms the rulers, the priests, the prophets, the idolatrous and adulterous masses. When Israel was young, Israel was faithful. Then God courted it and sanctified it as His people, sacred as the first fruit from the field of humanity. But Israel proved itself unworthy. Following after vulgar gods, it become a vulgar people. This is an astonishing thing, "an evil and bitter thing":

> Be astonished, O ye heavens, at this,
> And be horribly afraid, be ye exceeding amazed,
> Saith the Lord.
> For My people have committed two evils:
> They have forsaken Me, the fountain of
>   living waters,
> And hewed them out cisterns,
>   broken cisterns,
> That can hold no water.[16]

This noble vine turned into a degenerate plant. Raving mad with passion, like a young, wild ass, Israel turned prostitute. It is futile to attempt saving her from her *Baalim.* With idolatry went adultery and robbery:

Also in thy skirts is found the blood of the souls of the innocent poor.[17]

The depth of the tragedy is that the same Israel could become the ideal for all nations and the light of the world, if Israel only would. The prophet permits himself to dream

[16]2:12–13.   [17]2:34.

of his people returning to God in penitence. From the bare heights he hears supplicating voices:

> Here we are, we are come unto Thee;
> For Thou art the Lord our God.
> Truly vain have proved the hills,
> The uproar of the mountains;
> Truly in the Lord our God
> Is the salvation of Israel.[18]

The prophet's dream was only a dream.

> But this people hath a revolting and a rebellious heart;
> They are revolted, and gone.[19]

The rich grew fat and sleek on the misery of the poor; the prophets preached lies; the priests were only pious exploiters.

> For from the least of them even unto the greatest of them
> Every one is greedy for gain;
> And from the prophet even unto the priest
> Every one dealeth falsely.
> They have healed also the hurt of My people lightly,
> Saying: "Peace, peace," when there is no peace.[20]

> .   .   .   .

And my people love to have it so![21]

REFORMATION OF JOSIAH
621 B.C.

The Scythian scare was followed by the excitement of the Reformation of Josiah. This was the next major

[18]3:22–23.   [19]5:23.   [20]6:13–14.   [21]5:31.

event to touch the life of Jeremiah. The economic and social life of the nation was rocked along with the religious. The king himself led the revival. It was a noisy, violent day: the Temple ransacked, highways and mountain-tops searched for hidden shrines, altars smashed, sepulchres raided, bones of dead men scattered to the wind, priests slaughtered, idols burned. Religious zealots were having their fling for the Lord. Pious souls were gleefully smashing altars, and other pious souls were enraged. A national Passover was celebrated with all the pomp of an intricate ritual. Necromancers, soothsayers, witches were fleeing the land.

Just what part, if any, Jeremiah played in this revolution we do not know. The high pitch of emotion and tumult, the eloquence, deep piety, and lofty teachings of Deuteronomy must have won his support. That he was in close sympathy with much of the new legislation is obvious. The compassion and fervor of the legislator, reminiscent of Hosea, the belief in God as "the King of Kings and Lord of Lords" and in His government of the world, the conviction that Israel had entered into a covenant with Him to be His prophet among the nations, the condemnation of Israel's disloyalty to its God, the abolition of the local shrines, which Jeremiah saw everywhere and which he detested, the concentration of worship in one central sanctuary, the call to national repentance—with all these Jeremiah must have been in ardent sympathy.

With at least three aspects of Deuteronomic teaching Jeremiah probably differed. First, the religion legislated in Deuteronomy is national in character. It is the nation

that is called to its post of duty, the nation that is
loyal or disloyal, punished or rewarded; the individual,
on the whole, was submerged in the nation. Jeremiah's
thought was moving in the direction of the individual.
Not merely the nation but the individual soul as a
moral agent must make peace with its God. Secondly,
Deuteronomy is a law book; it is the legislator's approach
to religious belief and practice. It emphasizes ritual and
sacrifice. Jeremiah's sympathies were in the direction of
the ethical, spiritual, sincerity of worship rather than
accuracy of ritual. Like the rest of the prophets, he had
little use for ritual. He saw in it an impediment to the
realization of true religion. Thirdly, the divine government of the world, meting out rewards to the righteous
and punishment to the wicked in just measure, stated in
Deuteronomy as divinely revealed truth, harassed the
mind of Jeremiah. Like Job he searched for an answer
and could find none.

> Right wouldest Thou be, O Lord,
> Were I to contend with Thee,
> Yet will I reason with Thee:
> Wherefore doth the way of the wicked prosper?
> Wherefore are all they secure that deal
>   very treacherously?[22]

UNDER JEHOIAKIM
608–605 B.C.

Despair swept Judah upon the death of Josiah. That
was the third major event in the lifetime of Jeremiah.

---

[22]12:1. For a summary of Deuteronomy, see pages 86–92.

The people enthroned the slain monarch's son, Shallum, and expressed their confidence in him by changing his name to Jehoahaz, "the Lord hath taken hold." Three months later he was deposed by the man who had murdered his father, imprisoned, and finally deported to Egypt. Pharaoh Necho placed Jehoiakim, another son of Josiah, upon the throne. He was a willing puppet and petty tyrant with none of his father's lofty standards. For ten years (607–597) he bled his nation for the enrichment of his Egyptian and later Babylonian masters and his own glorification.

The Reformation of Josiah ended in failure. The God-fearing king was slain (when he was only thirty-nine years of age), his good son imprisoned, his unworthy son on the throne, the Egyptian yoke replaced the Assyrian. This was in the wake of national repentance and reform. Disillusionment gripped Judah. Where was God's just government of the world so eloquently announced in Deuteronomy? The nation relapsed into every idolatry. Jeremiah complains bitterly:

The children gather wood, and the fathers kindle the fire, and the women knead the dough, to make cakes to the queen of heaven, and to pour out drink-offerings unto other gods, that they may provoke Me.[23]

For the children of Judah have done that which is evil in My sight, saith the Lord; they have set their detestable things in the house whereon My name is called, to defile it. And they have built the high places of Topheth, which is in the valley of the son of Hinnom, to burn their sons and their daughters in the fire; which I commanded not, neither came it into My mind.[24]

[23]7:18.   [24]7:30–31.

The stork knows the time for return to warmer climes, but
Judah is too stupid to know how to return to the Lord.
The false pen of the scribes has done its evil work; it has
perverted the minds of the people.

> From the prophet even unto the priest
> Every one dealeth falsely.[25]

Jeremiah and Jehoiakim were in bitter and constant
conflict. The prophet opposed the king's alliance with
Egypt. He urged peace with Babylon. Egypt's sun had
set; there was no hope for Judah except in a covenant
of peace with the new world menace. Above all, Jeremiah
opposed the king's idolatry and perfidy. In his denunciation of the corrupt monarch Jeremiah rises to majestic
stature in attacking evil:

> Woe unto him that buildeth his house
>   by unrighteousness,
> And his chambers by injustice;
> That useth his neighbour's service
>   without wages,
> And giveth him not his hire;
> That saith: "I will build me
>   a wide house
> And spacious chambers,"
> And cutteth him out windows,
> And it is ceiled with cedar,
>   and painted with vermilion.
> Shalt thou reign, because thou
>   strivest to excel in cedar?
> Did not thy father eat and drink,
>   and do justice and righteousness?

[25] 8:10.

Then it was well with him.
He judged the cause of the poor and needy;
Then it was well.
Is not this to know Me? saith the Lord.

But thine eyes and thy heart
Are not but for thy covetousness,
And for shedding innocent blood,
And for oppression, and for violence,
    to do it.

Therefore thus saith the Lord concerning
Jehoiakim the son of Josiah, king of Judah:

They shall not lament for him:
"Ah my brother!" or: "Ah sister!"
They shall not lament for him:
"Ah lord!" or: "Ah his glory!"
He shall be buried with the burial
    of an ass,
Drawn and cast forth beyond the gates
    of Jerusalem.[26]

Jeremiah found himself attacked from every quarter. King and prophet could not live at peace in the same society. The established leadership, entrenched in the religious and social prerogatives of the time, the heedless masses forever relapsing into religious vice, roused the fires of rage in the breast of the prophet. His tongue was ready and merciless; he felt no fear and knew no restraint. Horrible visions haunted him—invasion, devastation, slaughter, the wrath of God—and he gave full expression to them in vivid symbolism and burning words.

[26] 22:13-19.

In the sight of God, Israel is like a rotten rag, filthy and useless.[27]

THE BROKEN BOTTLE

One day, sometime toward the end of the evil reign of Jehoiakim,[28] Jeremiah procured an earthen bottle, secured a number of respected elders to accompany him and proceeded to the valley of the son of Hinnom, there to dramatize the disaster that was to befall the nation. That valley was an infamous spot. There, bleaching in the sun, were heaps of infants' bones, sacrificial victims to Moloch. Josiah had sought to discredit this valley forever by defiling it in the most emphatic manner known to him, but it came back to its former prestige under the encouragement of his own son. From the name of this valley and its evil association the later rabbis derived the name Gehenna.

Bottle in hand, surrounded by conventionally respectable and accepted leaders, facing, quite likely, a curious crowd, Jeremiah unburdened himself of a bitter tirade:

And I will make void the counsel of Judah and Jerusalem in this place; and I will cause them to fall by the sword before their enemies, and by the hand of them that seek their life; and their carcasses will I give to be food for the fowls of the heaven, and for the beasts of the earth; and I will make this city an astonishment, and a hissing; every one that passeth thereby shall be astonished and hiss because of all the plagues thereof; and I will cause them to eat the flesh of their sons and the flesh of their daughters, and they shall eat every one the flesh

---

[27]13:1–11. This, apparently, reports an ecstatic experience rather than an actual event.

[28]The exact order of the biographic incidents cited here is not quite clear.

of his friend, in the siege and in the straitness, wherewith their enemies, and they that seek their life, shall straiten them.[29]

He flung the bottle to the ground, smashing it into a thousand fragments as he concluded:

Even so will I break this people and this city, as one breaketh a potter's vessel, that cannot be made whole again.[30]

Not satisfied with this performance, he proceeded to the Temple and there repeated his burden. The inevitable happened. He was seized by an official and imprisoned. The following morning he was freed. But Jeremiah did not take his leave before he heaped the curses of God upon the man who had imprisoned him. Was he not the prophet of the living God? Was it not God they were defying by persecuting him?[31]

TEMPLE SERMON AND PRISON

About the same time Jeremiah delivered his famous Temple sermon. There are two versions of this sermon.[32] Its theme was his constant burden; he must have repeated it over and over again.

There must have been considerable apprehension in Judah at the time this sermon was delivered. The nation was on the edge of a precipice. A decisive day was on the wing. The battle of Carchemish was rumbling in the distance. Babylon was to defeat Egypt and clamp down its brutal paw on Judah. The course of empire was shifting again. If the masses and their popular leaders were un-

[29]19:7–9.   [30]*Ibid.*, 11.   [31]19:14–20:6.   [32]7:1–28 and 26:1–9.

aware of it, Jeremiah's heart was pounding with apprehension. The masses were heedless, "trusting in lies." Their God was mighty; their armies were invincible. And was not this Temple His own house? Would not a mighty God defend His own tribe and His own earthly abode? The Temple was inviolable and Jerusalem was safe.

From all parts of Judah the crowds had come to the national shrine at Jerusalem to keep holiday. A large, excited crowd of peasants must have gathered about the prophet as he stood in some conspicuous spot, perhaps on the steps of the Temple, and spoke vehemently:

Hear the word of the Lord, all ye of Judah, that enter in at these gates to worship the Lord. Thus saith the Lord of hosts, the God of Israel: Amend your ways and your doings, and I will cause you to dwell in this place. Trust ye not in lying words, saying: "The temple of the Lord, the temple of the Lord, the temple of the Lord, are these." Nay, but if ye thoroughly amend your ways and your doings; if ye thoroughly execute justice between a man and his neighbour; if ye oppress not the stranger, the fatherless, and the widow, and shed not innocent blood in this place, neither walk after other gods to your hurt; then will I cause you to dwell in this place, in the land that I gave to your fathers, for ever and ever. Behold, ye trust in lying words, that cannot profit. Will ye steal, murder, and commit adultery, and swear falsely, and offer unto Baal, and walk after other gods whom ye have not known, and come and stand before Me in this house, whereupon My name is called, and say: "We are delivered," that ye may do all these abominations? Is this house, whereupon My name is called, become a den of robbers in your eyes? Behold, I, even I, have seen it, saith the Lord.[33]

[33] 7:2–11.

Shrines believed inviolable by the crowds have been reduced to ashes. That has happened and it will happen again. Jeremiah reminded his hearers of the fate of Shiloh. This sharpened the point to his predictions and stung his hearers into anger.

He was promptly arrested and court-martialled. The proceedings of the trial are told in reasonable detail.[34]

Priests, prophets and the mob leaped on Jeremiah with the cry of treason. It was an astounding utterance. The man is a traitor and must die. A court was quickly organized. It squatted "in the entry of the new gate of the Lord's house." Prosecuting him, demanding the death penalty, were the priests and the prophets. The princes, serving as justices, were more decent. They had retained a measure of respect for the man of God. The religious teachers had none.

Jeremiah's conduct before this court is one of the most heroic scenes in the Bible. It brings to mind Socrates' conduct before the Athenian jury. He does not back water; he does not equivocate; he does not beg for mercy; he does not engage in dramatics. For once he is not sorry for himself. He speaks with superb poise in the face of an enraged mob and their leaders:

Then spoke Jeremiah unto all the princes and to all the people, saying: "The Lord sent me to prophesy against this house and against this city all the words that ye have heard. Therefore now amend your ways and your doings, and hearken to the voice of the Lord your God; and the Lord will repent Him of the evil that He hath pronounced against you. But as for me, behold, I am in your hand; do with me as is good and right in your eyes.[35]

[34] 26.   [35] 26:12–14.

He succeeded in a measure. Some of the common people were moved by his piety, though their religious leaders continued clamoring for his life. Some one recalled the tradition of Micah the Morashtite. He, too, had spoken in a similar vein, yet he was not molested. The record of the trial ends abruptly. Jeremiah was convicted and sentenced to death. "Nevertheless," the chronicler reports, "the hand of Ahikam the son of Shaphan was with Jeremiah that they should not give him into the hand of the people to put him to death."[36]

BARUCH

Who were Jeremiah's friends at this time? Who shared his anguish? Who cheered him? Jeremiah speaks bitter words against his many enemies; he says nothing about his friends. Did he have none?

From the book of Jeremiah we learn that some friends he did have and that they did stand by him in the hours of his need. A number of the princes that constituted the court pleaded for him under trial for treason.[37] Were they friends or only just judges? A man by the name of Ahikam saved him when sentenced to die. Ahikam was an aged and trusted member of the nobility. He had served under Josiah and had retained something of the spirit of that righteous monarch. A number of the nobility pleaded with Jehoiakim to save Jeremiah's prophecies from the flames.[38] Later in his life we shall see an Ethiopian eunuch saving him from sure death by extricating him from a cistern.[39] He found men to carry his message to far-away Babylon.

[36]26:24.   [37]26:16.   [38]36:25.   [39]38:7-13.

But these were probably the chance kindnesses of good men. One friend who stood by him more than twenty long and cruel years, sharing the prophet's own moods and anguish, was Baruch, the son of Neriah.

Baruch was a member of the nobility. Attracted to Jeremiah, he renounced his prerogatives as a member of the aristocracy and followed the lamenting prophet. It is to Baruch that we are indebted for the preservation of the utterances of Jeremiah. It was he who wrote them down upon Jeremiah's dictation and thus produced the first draft of what came to be the present book of Jeremiah.

Just when the two men met we do not know. But we do know that by the year 604-603 B.C. when Baruch read the prophecies of Jeremiah in the Temple, he was recognized as Jeremiah's friend and scribe. We see Baruch by Jeremiah's side in every subsequent crisis in the life of the prophet—in his feud with Jehoiakim, during the last siege of Jerusalem, among the Judeans left behind, in exile in Egypt.

CARCHEMISH AND THE END
605–586 B.C.

Came the year 605 and sealed the fate of southwestern Asia for the next century. Judah and its puppet king were dragged in the gale. That was the fourth turning point in the life-time of Jeremiah.

Jehoiakim had come to the throne and maintained himself in power by the favor of Pharaoh Necho. Now he was the vassal of the Babylonian whom he had defied. Pharaoh Necho, in Jeremiah's phrase, was "but a noise."

For three years Jehoiakim dutifully paid tribute to

his Babylonian master. Then he defaulted, probably incited by new flirtations on the part of discredited Egypt.
Nebuchadrezzar promptly unleashed bands of Arameans,
Moabites, Ammonites, and finally the Babylonian legions
against Judah. Merciful death saved Jehoiakim. He died
in the year 597 B.C., just as the Babylonian armies were
approaching Jerusalem.[40] Jeremiah's prophecy seems to
have been vindicated. The prophet had predicted that he
would be "buried with the burial of an ass, drawn and
cast forth beyond the gates of Jerusalem."[41]

JEREMIAH WRITES DOWN HIS PROPHECIES

As the nation was thus drifting to its ruin under
Jehoiakim, Jeremiah decided to reduce his utterances to
writing. This he did in the wake of the battle of Carchemish. The prophet was now overwhelmingly convinced of
the rightness of his convictions and desperate that so little
heed was given him. He dictated to his friend Baruch the
prophecies he had spoken over a period of twenty-two
years and directed him to read them in the Temple. About
a year later Baruch found his opportunity.[42]

The nation was observing a fast. The Temple was
crowded with Judean peasants come from all parts of the
country. The nobility and the army, the priests and the
prophets were there. "Then read Baruch from the book
the words of Jeremiah . . . in the ears of all the people."

Baruch was promptly summoned before a group of influential princes. Scroll in hand he presented himself.
The Bible report is vivid:

[40]II Kings 23:31–24:5. A slightly different version of Jehoiakim's end
is given in II Chron. 36:6.
[41]22:19.   [42]36.

And they said unto him: "Sit down now, and read it in our ears." So Baruch read it in their ears. Now it came to pass, when they had heard all the words, they turned in fear one toward another, and said unto Baruch: "We will surely tell the king of all these words." And they asked Baruch, saying: "Tell us now: How didst thou write all these words at his mouth?" Then Baruch answered them: "He pronounced all these words unto me with his mouth, and I wrote them with ink in the book." Then said the princes unto Baruch: "Go, hide thee, thou and Jeremiah; and let no man know where ye are." And they went in to the king into the court; but they had deposited the roll in the chamber of Elishama the scribe; and they told all the words in the ears of the king.[43]

The king, enraged, ordered the scroll to be brought and read before him.

Now the king was sitting in the winter-house in the ninth month; and the brazier was burning before him. And it came to pass, when Jehudi had read three or four columns, that he cut it with the penknife, and cast it into the fire that was in the brazier, until all the roll was consumed in the fire that was in the brazier.[44]

In vain did a number of those present beg the monarch to save the document. The book was burned and orders went out that both Jeremiah and Baruch be fetched before the king. The Bible historian adds quaintly: "But the Lord hid them."

Thus was the first draft of the book of Jeremiah made and destroyed. Fortunately, the prophet would not yield to defeat. He summoned Baruch again and dictated his prophecies anew, expressing them in even more vigorous

[43]36:15–20.   [44]36:22–23.

words, heaping further curses on the head of Jehoiakim. "And there were added besides unto them many like words."

We are afforded a glimpse into Baruch's own personality at this time. A brief passage[45] describes the deep despondency that came over him as a result of the king's conduct. His lifework was undone; his sacrifices were futile.

> Woe is me now!
> For the Lord hath added sorrow to my pain;
> I am weary with my groaning,
> I find no rest.

The despondent Jeremiah was forced to comfort him. They were in the depths of a cruel age. How might one expect great things for himself? Enough that one's life was spared. God Himself was forced to destroy the work of His own hands.

THE BEGINNING OF THE END

The blow aimed at Jehoiakim struck his son and successor, Jehoiachin. The boy was only eighteen years old when he came to the throne in an hour of severe crisis. He reigned three months when Nebuchadrezzar besieged Jerusalem. That was the beginning of the end, the last major event in the history of Judah that weaves the background to the life of Jeremiah. The young king capitulated. Accompanied by the queen-mother, his wives and his advisers, he placed himself and his country at the mercy of the invaders. He was chained and deported to

Babylon, where he languished in prison for thirty-seven years.

The city and the Temple were plundered in the year 597 B.C. Ten thousand captives—the young, the able, the craftsmen—were carried off to Babylon; among them was the prophet Ezekiel. Left behind were the aged, the sick, the crippled, the helpless and hopeless. "None remained, save the poorest sort of the people of the land."[46] Zedekiah, twenty-one-year-old lad, uncle of the exiled Jehoiachin, was appointed king over the decimated country and ragged remnant. He took office by swearing allegiance to Nebuchadrezzar. No king of Judah ever faced so hopeless a situation. For ten years he struggled against overwhelming odds and finally was caught and crushed in the collapse of Judah.

In far-away Babylon the prophet Ezekiel spoke contemptuously of Zedekiah. He was weak, lacking courage to rule and lacking courage to rebel.

> There is in her (Judah) no strong rod
> To be a sceptre to rule.[47]

He had no domestic program, no foreign policy, no resources and no experience. Famine and pestilence ravaged the miserable population. Marauding bands harassed it from every side. What could Zedekiah do even if he did have the will to act?

THE YOKE

Jeremiah remained in Jerusalem, amidst its ruins, in the thick of its misery. His conduct was consistent with the

[46] II Kings 24:14. According to Jer. 52:28 this convoy numbered only 3023.
[47] Ezek. 19:14.

views he had urged on unwilling ears over many years.
Once and forever Judah must realize that there is no
salvation in alliances with Egypt. Submission to Nebuchadrezzar was the only course open to the stricken nation.
Not that he had any affection for Babylon; Babylon was
only the cruel agent fulfilling God's unfathomable will.
In time the conqueror would himself be conquered.

> For Israel is not widowed, nor Judah,
> Of his God, of the Lord of hosts.[48]

But for the time she was God's instrument and Judah
must submit.

On three separate occasions Jeremiah gave forceful
expression to his conviction,[49] challenging vehemently the
sorcerers, diviners, soothsayers, and false prophets who
would mislead the people with false hopes. To five different kings, plotting rebellion against Nebuchadrezzar,
he sent wooden yokes. To Zedekiah, too, he sent one with
the admonition:

Bring your necks into the yoke of the king of Babylon
and serve him and his people and live. Why will ye die,
thou and thy people, by the sword, by the famine, by
pestilence . . . ?[50]

He himself seems to have gone about the ruins of Jerusalem and its distracted population with twisted bars in
the shape of a yoke around his neck. A militant advocate
of rebellion against Babylon, a man by the name of
Hananiah, seized and broke this yoke. A crowd stood by
and watched. Jeremiah left the scene dejected, but soon

[48] 51:5. See verses 59–64. [49] 27, 28, 29. [50] 27:12–13.

made emphatic reply: the bars of iron will replace the bars of wood.

To the exiles in Babylon he wrote a letter urging them to ignore the prophets of lies, make peace with their new environment, and settle down to a normal life.

Build ye houses, and dwell in them, and plant gardens, and eat the fruit of them; take ye wives, and beget sons and daughters; and take wives for your sons, and give your daughters to husbands, that they may bear sons and daughters; and multiply ye there, and be not diminished. And seek the peace of the city whither I have caused you to be carried away captive, and pray unto the Lord for it; for in the peace thereof shall ye have peace.[51]

ZEDEKIAH REBELS

In 589 B.C. a new king came to the throne of Egypt, and the anti-Babylonian policy was resumed with new vigor. Zedekiah joined in the new intrigues. Nebuchadrezzar and his legions were immediately on the march westward. Judah lay helpless before them; Jerusalem was once again like a bird shut up in a cage.[52]

Jeremiah urged immediate surrender.[53] Why burn a city and murder its population? They had rebelled against God and man. Resistance was useless. Zedekiah spurned this advice. Perhaps the zealots in his own camp would not permit him to heed it. A wave of piety swept the Holy City—a frantic attempt to win God's favor. Masters actually released their Hebrew slaves whom they had been holding in violation of the law. But that was only impulsive piety. As soon as word reached Jerusalem that an Egyptian army was on the way to help repel the enemy,

[51]29:5-7.   [52]II Kings 25.   [53]Jer. 34.

the religious reformation was immediately reversed and the slaves were brought back into subjection. Jeremiah's voice was heard in stern reproof. How could he keep his peace when such perfidy was enacted before his very eyes by the leading men of the nation?

Therefore thus saith the Lord: Ye have not hearkened unto Me, to proclaim liberty, every man to his brother, and every man to his neighbour; behold, I proclaim for you a liberty, saith the Lord, unto the sword, unto the pestilence, and unto the famine; and I will make you a horror unto all the kingdoms of the earth.[54]

Nebuchadrezzar was compelled to divert his fighting forces to check the Egyptian expedition. That gave Jerusalem a breathing spell. Wild joy swept the city. Jeremiah stood utterly discredited. He was a frantic, false prophet and a traitor. Still he persisted in his views and went about the city speaking his mind:

Deceive not yourselves, saying: "The Chaldeans will surely depart from us," for they will not depart. For though ye had smitten the whole army of the Chaldeans that fight against you, and there were left but wounded men among them, yet would they rise up every man in his tent, and burn this city with fire.[55]

Jeremiah had reached the very depths of disfavor. Contempt must have stared at him from every face he met; every look men, women, and children gave him must have sent a chill through his heart. On the way to his native Anathoth one day, as he was attempting to pass through the city gate, he was arrested, beaten, and thrown

[54]34:17.　　　　[55]37:9–10

into a cesspool.[56] He was a deserter, surrendering to the enemy! "And in the cistern there was no water, but mire; and Jeremiah sank in the mire." Salvation came through an Ethiopian eunuch employed in the palace, Ebed-melech by name. He hurried to the king and secured permission to rescue the prophet. A number of men were instructed to assist him. The Bible describes the rescue:

So Ebed-melech took the men with him, and went into the house of the king under the treasury, and took thence worn clouts and worn rags, and let them down by cords into the pit to Jeremiah. And Ebed-melech the Ethiopian said unto Jeremiah: "Put now these worn clouts and rags under thine armholes under the cords." And Jeremiah did so. So they drew up Jeremiah with the cords, and took him up out of the pit; and Jeremiah remained in the court of the guard.[57]

KING AND PROPHET IN THE DEPTHS OF NIGHT

Zedekiah had a superstitious respect for Jeremiah. He could not live with him and could not entirely forget him. His own position was desperate. Why way lay salvation? Which way was he to turn? The enemy was storming the gates of his city, the last stronghold of his nation; the Egyptian, as always, was "but a noise," a broken staff upon which one could not lean; his own ministry was torn with dissension and divided counsel; his people were mad and perishing; his prophets were only flattering flunkies. There was no vision from the Lord. Jeremiah was the only man he feared and respected, but his advice was surrender! If God would only speak! But his God was invisible. He was in the high heavens. Of what good is an invisible God in the high heavens? How may one talk with Him? How may one implore Him? But Jeremiah spoke in His name. Jeremiah was in touch with Him.

In the depth of night, in fear of his own counsellors, Zedekiah sent for Jeremiah. The Bible account is colorful:

Then Zedekiah the king sent, and took Jeremiah the prophet unto him into the third entry that was in the house of the Lord; and the king said unto Jeremiah: "I will ask thee a thing; hide nothing from me." Then Jeremiah said unto Zedekiah: "If I declare it unto thee, wilt thou not surely put me to death? and if I give thee counsel, thou wilt not hearken unto me." So Zedekiah the king swore secretly unto Jeremiah, saying: "As the Lord liveth, that made us this soul, I will not put thee to death, neither will I give thee into the hand of these men that seek thy life."

Then said Jeremiah unto Zedekiah: "Thus saith the Lord, the God of hosts, the God of Israel: If thou wilt go forth unto the king of Babylon's princes, then thy soul shall live, and this city shall not be burned with fire; and thou shalt live, thou, and thy house; but if thou wilt not go forth to the king of Babylon's princes, then shall this city be given into the hand of the Chaldeans, and they shall burn it with fire, and thou shalt not escape out of their hand."

Then said Zedekiah unto Jeremiah: "Let no man know these words, and thou shalt not die. But if the princes hear that I have talked with thee, and they come unto thee, and say unto thee: Declare unto us now what thou hast said unto the king; hide it not from us, and we will not put thee to death; also what the king said unto thee; then thou shalt say unto them: I presented my supplication before the king, that he would not cause me to return to Jonathan's house, to die there.[58]

[58]38:14–18; . . . 24–26.

Zedekiah yielded to the clamor of the fanatic patriots and defied Babylon. The battering-rams of Babylon and their deadly archers immediately besieged Jerusalem. For a year and a half the siege lasted—a year and a half of insane heroism within the walls of Jerusalem.

To the harried population the conduct of the discredited Jeremiah was probably beneath contempt. Having consistently wailed his lamentation and urged surrender, at this desperate hour he dramatized his conviction that Jerusalem would be restored and Judah rehabilitated! He expressed it in characteristically symbolic manner.

A cousin came to him informing him that some land owned by his family in Anathoth would revert to him if he redeemed it. The man who had refused to marry and bring a family into the world because of his overpowering conviction that the world was doomed, the man who had urged and pleaded with Zedekiah to surrender to the invader at the gates, and cursed him for not taking his advice, redeemed the land and took special pain to preserve the deed for many years to come as an expression of his hope for his Judah and Jerusalem. In the presence of witnesses he charged Baruch:

Thus saith the Lord of hosts, the God of Israel: Take these deeds, this deed of purchase, both that which is sealed, and this deed which is open, and put them in an earthen vessel; that they may continue many days. For thus saith the Lord of hosts, the God of Israel: Houses and fields and vineyards shall yet again be bought in this land.[59]

The maddened population could hardly be expected to

[59] 32:14–15.

see the long-range view Jeremiah took and how consistent
it was with the preachment of his lifetime. Jeremiah himself was torn by doubt. Would Judah be restored? Would
the night of exile be followed by a new morn? An inner
voice steadies his fears. God is faithful. "Behold I will
gather them out of all the countries. . . . I will bring
them back unto this place and I will cause them to dwell
safely."[60]

He had hardly completed the ceremony of depositing
the deed when the Egyptian army upon which Jerusalem
relied reversed its course and beat a hasty retreat. The
siege was intensified. Jeremiah appeared a ridiculous, insane figure.

In the summer of 586 B.C. the north gate of Jerusalem
yielded to the pounding of the battering-rams. A breach
was effected. The tide of invasion poured into the city.
Under cover of night Zedekiah, his family, and his guard
fled the city. They were overtaken. The tragic Zedekiah
saw his own sons slaughtered by the Babylonians. His own
eyes were pulled out of their sockets. In chains he was
taken prisoner to Babylon.

Jerusalem must never rebel again. Seventy-three of her
distinguished citizens were hacked to pieces as Nebuchadrezzar watched. A larger group, in chains, were brought
before a military court at Riblah to receive various sentences. Among these was Jeremiah.

Was he not a friend of Babylon? Had he not advised
surrender to the Babylonians? How was the marauder to
understand the heart and mind of the prophet? Neither
did he know of the scroll which Jeremiah had ordered tied

[60]32:36 ff.

to a stone and sent to the bottom of the Euphrates as a symbol of the prophet's conviction: "Thus shall Babylon sink, and shall not rise, because of the evil that I am bringing upon her."[61] The choice was given him to go to Babylon or to remain in Jerusalem. He preferred to remain in Jerusalem amidst its ruins and among the ragged remnants of the population.

Jerusalem was systematically plundered. The ablebodied were transported. An end had come to Judah, to Jerusalem, to the Temple. Judah was in ashes.

But among the exiles by the waters of Babylon a miracle was wrought. From its own ashes Judah, the phœnix of mankind, arose reborn and reconsecrated. The doom pronounced upon Babylon by Jeremiah was rumbling in the distance. Again the course of empire was shifting. Soon there were heard in the Judean colonies new enchanting voices, especially those of the priest-prophet Ezekiel and that of the poet-prophet whose poems are embodied in the book of Isaiah. From the distant heights came ringing the glad tidings: "Behold your God."

What happened to the aged Jeremiah? His last days were a horrible procession of murder among the dire population. He who had foretold misery without end was now compelled to speak words of comfort. Gedaliah, the governor appointed by Nebuchadrezzar, was assassinated by one who sought the throne of devastated Judah. The population was in terror of the new reprisals and panicky in attempts to escape to Egypt. Jeremiah pleaded against it but in vain. The tide had set in and he himself was swept along. In Egypt—the Egypt he hated and had cursed

[61] 51:59–64.

throughout his life—surrounded by cynical fellow Judeans who were contemptuously denying everything he had preached throughout his martyred life[62] he disappeared from view, scorned and derided of men.

CONTROLLING IDEALS

1. *"Thou Hast Enticed Me"*

The teachings and the personalities of the prophets were one and inseparable. This is particularly true of Jeremiah. His tragic figure palpitates with the dreams, hopes and fears that spelled the burden of his soul.

All the heroic qualities that characterize the personalities of the literary prophets find their fullest development in Jeremiah. The hand of the Lord had touched his mouth in his youth. Henceforth he was a transfigured person. That was at the root of his soul, the cause of his external strife, inner conflict, his moodiness, his occasional trances. This divine compulsion it was that made him a fearless denouncer of evil in high places. That it was, too, that transformed his despair into hope. From the world and its cruelties he turned to God. From God he turned to God and found peace in the shadow of His wings. In one of the most revealing and touching passages in prophetic literature, Jeremiah lays bare the burden of his heart:

> O Lord, Thou hast enticed me,
>   and I was enticed,
> Thou hast overcome me, and
>   hast prevailed;

[62]44:15–30.

I am become a laughing-stock
    all the day,
Every one mocketh me,
For as often as I speak,
    I cry out,
I cry: "Violence and spoil";
Because the word of the Lord
    is made
A reproach unto me, and a
    derision, all the day.
And if I say: "I will not make
    mention of Him,
Nor speak any more in His name,"
Then there is in my heart as it were
    a burning fire
Shut up in my bones,
And I weary myself to hold it in,
But cannot.[63]

2. *Beyond Despair*

A deep, dark shadow of gloom follows the personality
of Jeremiah. His utterances are lamentations for the dead
and the dying. But Jeremiah was a man of faith. He
saw beyond despair. If a rotten world was collapsing and
a degraded humanity was tobogganing to disaster, in the
shadow was God. His everlasting love will not fail. Hence
hope triumphs over despair.

"From afar the Lord appeared unto me."
"Yea, I have loved thee with an everlasting love;
Therefore with affection have I drawn thee.
Again I will build, and thou shalt
    be built,
O virgin of Israel;

[63]20:7–9. See also 20:10–12; 11:18–23; 12:6; 15:10; 17:15–18; 18:18.

Again shalt thou be adorned with
    thy tabrets,
And shalt go forth in the dances
    of them that make merry.
Again shalt thou plant vineyards
    upon the mountains of Samaria;
The planters shall plant, and shall
    have the use thereof.
For there shall be a day,
That the watchmen shall call upon
    the mount Ephraim:
Arise ye, and let us go up to Zion,
Unto the Lord our God."

For thus saith the Lord:
Sing with gladness for Jacob,
And shout at the head of the nations;
Announce ye, praise ye, and say:
"O Lord, save Thy people,
The remnant of Israel."[64]

3. *The Potter and the Clay*

One day Jeremiah found himself observing a potter shaping a vessel. He watches the clay yielding to the pressure of the potter's fingers and the revolving wheels. Gradually the clay is assuming form. The potter examines his work critically at intervals; he exerts pressure where it is needed. But the vessel is lopsided. It is faulty. Not that is what the potter wishes to produce. He therefore crushes the misshapen thing into one lump and applies it to the revolving wheel anew. A thought flashes through the mind of the prophet. As the potter reshapes his vessel in the effort to give it more perfect form, so does God recreate humanity in keeping with His vision.

[64]31:3–7.

Then the word of the Lord came to me, saying: "O house of Israel, cannot I do with you as this potter? saith the Lord. Behold, as the clay in the potter's hand, so are ye in My hand, O house of Israel. At one instant I may speak concerning a nation, and concerning a kingdom, to pluck up and to break down and to destroy it; but if that nation turn from their evil, because of which I have spoken against it, I repent of the evil that I thought to do unto it. . . ."[65]

The Supreme Artist is trying to shape a more just humanity in a more righteous world. The rise and fall of nations, the social upheavals, the cruelty and the misery of the world, sorrow and frustration in the life of the individual are but the pressure He is exerting in fashioning the better world.

Israel is not doomed forever. Disciplined, it will return to the Lord a nobler people. Mother Rachel, weeping for the children who have either deserted her or were snatched from her, hears voices of comfort:

> Thus saith the Lord:
> Refrain thy voice from weeping,
> And thine eyes from tears;
> For thy work shall be rewarded,
>   saith the Lord;
> And they shall come back
>   from the land of the enemy.[66]

4. *The New Covenant*

Days are coming when Israel will return to itself. Then a new covenant will be effected between God and His

[65]18:5–8.   [66]31:16.

people. Upon the heart of man will this covenant be in-scribed. At last Israel will be faithful and worthy:

This is the covenant that I will make with the house of Israel after those days, saith the Lord, I will put My law in their inward parts, and in their heart will I write it; and I will be their God, and they shall be My people; and they shall teach no more every man his neighbour, and every man his brother, saying: "Know the Lord"; for they shall all know Me, from the least of them unto the greatest of them, saith the Lord; for I will forgive their iniquity, and their sin will I remember no more.[67]

This is perhaps the greatest contribution that Jeremiah made to the development of Judaism. Making religion the aspiration after God on the part of the individual heart and conscience, rather than an external discipline or a national cultus, Jeremiah gave impetus to the spiritual and the universal.

This heroic hope lured Jeremiah and sustained him. All the chaos and degradation of his time could not blur the vision, for Jeremiah lived by faith.

[67]31:33–34.

X

"BY THE WATERS OF BABYLON"

*How shall we sing the Lord's song
In a foreign land?*

PSALM 137:4.

JERUSALEM was a heap of ruins. The Temple was in ashes. Judah lay prostrate, her sons and daughters scattered throughout the towns and wastelands between the Tigris-Euphrates valley and the Nile. Where once men and women lived and loved, where children played, Psalmists worshipped, prophets spoke in lofty accents, there beasts prowled for human prey and vultures gorged themselves on human bodies. Men from distant cities, dressed in garments of mourning, brought offerings to Jerusalem and placed their sacrifices on the heaps of debris that was once the invincible sanctuary of the Almighty—a tragic expression of undying loyalty. Bands of marauders swept Jerusalem and Judah.

> How doth the city sit solitary,
> That was full of people!
> How is she become as a widow!
> She that was great among the nations,
> And princes among the provinces,
> How is she become tributary!
> She weepeth sore in the night,
> And her tears are on her cheeks;

144

> She hath none to comfort her
> Among all her lovers;
> All her friends have dealt treacherously
>   with her,
> They have become her enemies.[1]

God himself had deserted His own. More than that, He was now the enemy of Israel. Passionate words of inspired prophets of former days woke bitter memories. They had rebelled against God; they had sinned. Inciting visions of the false prophets led them astray; the idolatry round about them seduced them.

> Jerusalem hath grievously sinned,
> Therefore she is become as one unclean.[2]
> The crown is fallen from her head;
> Woe unto us! for we have sinned.[3]

Some of the population fled to the surrounding country, especially Egypt. They settled mainly in the fortress cities of Tahpanhes and Migdol, also in Memphis and Pathros. A large Jewish military colony flourished in Elephantine in Upper Egypt, an important frontier post, where a Temple to Jahu was maintained in defiance of the Deuteronomic law. There they abandoned themselves in cynical worship of whatever gods there were. What had the God of the prophets to offer them? Had He not failed them? Had He not sent confusion into their minds and pain into their hearts? They had nothing but contempt for the aged Jeremiah and his invisible God. Most assuredly they would worship the queen of heaven. As long as they were loyal to her, they "had plenty of food and

[1]Lam. 1:8 (1:1–2).   [2]Lam 1:8.   [3]Lam. 5:16.

were well and saw no evil. But since we left off to offer to the queen of heaven and to pour out drink offerings to her, we have wanted all things and have been consumed by the sword and by famine."[4]

A second sector of the population—about three fourths of the inhabitants—remained on the soil of Judah. They were the poorest of the land, as we have seen. They were not worth transporting and had not the initiative to flee nor the energy to rebel. A pitiful picture of famine, devastation, looting and plague is given in the scroll of Lamentations. Allowing for the imagination and the general spiritual excitement of the poet, the historic facts that form the background to this scroll are appalling. Ammonites, Moabites, Philistines, and particularly Edomites swarmed over the land like a storm of devouring locusts. "A half century later almost the whole of Judah's territory belonged to these invaders, and the bitter hatred of the Edomites, which finds expression in later times, dates from this period of encroachment."[5]

A third group of the Judean population were led captive to Babylon. These, as we have noted, were the choice of the people—the artisans, the priests, the military, the aristocracy, the able-bodied and mentally vigorous who might be expected to incite to rebellion if left in Judah and who might enrich the conqueror if taken to Babylon. They probably considered themselves as the true Israel and viewed with scorn the rabble back home. It is from the ranks of these that came the saving remnant of Judah, who rebuilt the sanctuary and restored the state. How

[4]Jer. 44:17–18.
[5]H. P. Smith, *Old Testament History*, p. 300.

many were taken to Babylon is not known. Estimates made by historians vary.[6]

> That bitter and impetuous nation
> That march through the breadth of the earth,
> To possess dwelling-places that are not theirs,

as the prophet Habakkuk had characterized the Babylonians, had done their work well. The Jew was now on his road of exile.

> By the rivers of Babylon,
> There we sat down, yea, we wept,
> When we remembered Zion.
> Upon the willows in the midst thereof
> We hanged up our harps.
> For there they that led us captive
>   asked of us words of song,
> And our tormentors asked of us mirth:
> "Sing us one of the songs of Zion."
>
> How shall we sing the Lord's song
> In a foreign land?
> If I forget thee, O Jerusalem,
> Let my right hand forget her cunning.
> Let my tongue cleave to the roof of
>   my mouth,
> If I remember thee not;
> If I set not Jerusalem
> Above my chiefest joy.[7]

Nebuchadrezzar was enlightened in his treatment of conquered peoples. His policy was deportation. That pre-

---

[6] I. M. Price estimates the number as close to 50,000 (*Dramatic Story of the Old Testament*, p. 359); Adolphe Lods places it at 20,000 (*The Prophets and the Rise of Judaism*, p. 174). Note the Biblical figures cited by these scholars.

[7] Ps. 137.

vented rebellion when his back was turned, and it brought
new human resources to the mighty empire he was building. His attitude toward the Judean exiles was liberal.
They were settled in the very heart of the New Babylonian
Empire, in the Tigris-Euphrates basin. With its abund-
ance of water, extensive irrigation system and network of
canals, it was one of the richest agricultural regions in
the world.

They were not only allowed promising soil where to
sink their roots and normalize their lives, but were given
the freedom to engage in commerce as well. Some of them
rose to wealth and power. Some were trained in the court
for diplomatic service, as the book of Daniel testifies. In
the course of the century they were able to send large
sums of money to finance the reconstruction of the Temple.[8] Religiously, too, they were free to shape their own
destinies, as far as the new landscape permitted them.
They could retain whatever family or tribal institutions
they pleased; they might educate their children in whatever customs they saw fit to preserve in the new world.

"HOW SHALL WE SING THE LORD'S SONG IN A STRANGE LAND?"

Grave problems confronted these exiles. They were in
a new civilization. Their own country, now reduced to a
Babylonian province, was small, provincial, stony; their
new home was spacious, fertile, cosmopolitan. They were
in the generous lap of the greatest empire on earth.
Gorgeous processions to the gods, military displays, the
riotous pageantry of an empire drunk with its own power,

[8]Ezra 2:68–69; 8:26–27; Nehem. 7:70–72.

captivated them. Temples to Marduk, Bel, Ishtar, Shamash towered majestically to the high heavens; from scores of ziggurats came calls to sacred orgies. The new climate was enervating, seducing. Their children were growing up more Babylonian than Hebrew. How might they hold their own children true to the God of their fathers? When, before the century had run its course, permission was given these refugees, who at one time wept so bitterly by the waters of Babylon, to return to their native land and rebuild their shrine to the God of their fathers, the overwhelming majority refused to budge. Only a small band returned to Zion.

How might they worship their God? They could not build a new Temple to His holy Name in the valley of the Euphrates. That was prohibited in the Deuteronomic legislation. Only in that place which God had chosen—Jerusalem—might the central shrine be built; only there might sacrifices be offered; only the authorized priests might officiate. But Jerusalem, the Temple, the accredited priesthood were no more.

And how might they still the gnawing remorse that Judah had brought this calamity on itself? And how might they silence the rising skepticism in the justice of God? It was their fathers that had sinned. Why was their particular generation punished?

> Our fathers have sinned, and are not;
> And we have borne their iniquities.[9]

The masses were in deep despair. "Our transgressions and our sins are upon us, and we pine away in them; how

[9]Lam. 5:7.

then should we live?"[10] Their central problem was nothing less than how to save themselves from inner dissolution, now that their external ties had snapped. "How shall we sing the Lord's song in a strange land?"

[10]Ezek. 33:10.

XI

EZEKIEL

---

*And He said unto me, Son of Man, stand upon
thy feet, and I will speak unto thee.*

EZEKIEL 2:1.

IN THE year 593 B.C.—in the fifth year of the captivity
—the heavens opened and a rush of strange, fantastic
visions overwhelmed an extraordinary soul. Henceforth
the hand of God rested upon Ezekiel, consecrating him
as "watchman" over his brethren in exile. A faithful
watchman he remained, warning, exhorting, directing
and consoling the conscience of his people. His was the
most remarkable ministry in the history of Judaism. He
breathed new spirit into the dry bones of his people and
made them alive with the vision of God.

Ezekiel has been described as "priest rather than
prophet," as "priest-prophet," as "pastor rather than
prophet," and as "pastor as well as prophet." He has
been called "the prophet of reconstruction," and "the
father of Judaism." That he suffered from violent mental
agitations, sinking into trances and seeing visions unknown to normal minds, every chapter of his book testifies.
He saw things that never were and never could be, neither
in the heavens above nor on the earth below nor in the

151

waters beneath the earth. Nevertheless, a distinguished
scholar states, and many competent scholars concur, that
he was "the most influential man that we find in the whole
course of Hebrew history."[1]

Strange and fantastic is his inaugural vision.[2] How
else shall we explain it except on the basis of trance?
Overwhelmed by a power beyond himself the prophet has
a most extraordinary experience. A furious storm tears
the heavens into shreds. Lightning flashes; a "great
cloud," with glowing embers in its lap, is swaying over
his head. Out of the cosmic chaos gradually emerges the
moving throne of God. Four creatures stand revealed.
Each has four wings and four faces—the face of a man,
a lion, an ox, and an eagle. Their legs are straight, like
those of a human being; but they terminate in the sole
of a calf and shine like burnished bronze. The dazed
prophet stares and the vision keeps on unfolding itself.
Under the wings he observes human hands. The creatures
move smoothly, in straight lines, never making a curve
or cutting an angle. Burning torches seem to be playing
among the figures. At their feet are wheels, topaz in color,
which move as the creatures move; over their heads a
firmament glistens like transparent ice. The wings come
into harmony and unity as they touch the firmament.
"And when they moved, I heard the noise of their wings
like the noise of great waters, like the voice of the Almighty. . . ." Beyond and above it all emerges, in faint
outline, a throne made of sapphire. The prophet falls to

[1] H. P. Smith, *Old Testament History*, p. 327.   [2] 1–3:21.

the ground overwhelmed. A voice haunts him: "Son of man, stand upon thy feet, and I will speak unto thee."

If this vision is strange and unearthly, baffling the normal mind, the commission that comes to the prophet is clear and convincing:

Son of man, I send thee to the children of Israel, to rebellious nations, that have rebelled against Me; they and their fathers have transgressed against Me, even unto this very day; and the children are brazen-faced and stiff-hearted, I do send thee unto them; and thou shalt say unto them: "Thus saith the Lord God." And they, whether they will hear, or whether they will forbear—for they are a rebellious house—yet shall know that there hath been a prophet among them.[3]

Like the prophets before him, especially his immediate predecessor, Jeremiah, Ezekiel must take his position and hold his ground against all the world. The classes will fight him; the masses will deride him. His duty, however, is clear. One power—and one power alone—he must obey: God.

Ecstasy overpowers him again:

And thou, son of man, hear what I say unto thee: be not thou rebellious like that rebellious house; open thy mouth, and eat that which I give thee. And when I looked, behold, a hand was put forth unto me; and, lo, a roll of a book was therein; and He spread it before me, and it was written within and without; and there was written therein lamentations, and moaning, and woe.

And He said unto me: "Son of man, eat that which thou findest; eat this roll, and go, speak unto the house of Israel." So I opened my mouth, and He caused me

[3]2:3-5.

to eat that roll. And He said unto me: "Son of man, cause thy belly to eat, and fill thy bowels with this roll that I give thee." Then did I eat it; and it was in my mouth as honey for sweetness.[4]

Carried by his vision, he proceeds to his appointed task. His place is among his fellow exiles: "Then a spirit lifted me up, and I heard behind me the voice of a great rushing: 'Blessed be the glory of the Lord from His place.' "[5]

The hand of God rests upon him. He is a person transformed. His duty is clear and compelling. He must serve as "watchman" over the house of Israel. He must warn of danger, exhort against evil. He must also console the righteous and allay the fears of the faithful.

So thou, son of man, I have set thee a watchman over the house of Israel; therefore, when thou shalt hear the word at My mouth, warn them from Me.[6]

He must be an honest and faithful watchman. He must not shut his eyes to danger; he must not pipe vain hopes. As faithful watchman he must live and think in a watch-tower, high above the tumult, the confusion, and the despair of the crowds. His vision must range over the whole landscape; his horizon must not be cramped. At the same time, he must be among the masses, be one of them, sharing their sorrows and experiencing their woes. He must be at one with them in everything but their sins and their follies. His is the responsibility to speak the word of God. Shifting the figure of speech, he speaks of himself as a shepherd whom God has appointed to guide

[4] 2:8—3:3.   [5] 3:12.   [6] 33:7.

his scattered flock. "My sheep wandered through all the mountains, and upon every high hill; yea, upon all the face of the earth were my sheep scattered, and there was none that did search or seek."[7] Bitterly he inveighs against the selfish shepherds who fatten themselves and allow their flock to drift to destruction:

The weak have ye not strengthened, neither have ye healed that which was sick, neither have ye bound up that which was broken, neither have ye brought back that which was driven away, neither have ye sought that which was lost; but with force have ye ruled over them and with rigour. So were they scattered, because there was no shepherd; and they became food to all the beasts of the field, and were scattered.[8]

Who was this strange person? Whence came his power? What direction did he give to the faith of his people?

THE SPIRITUAL CLIMATE OF HIS YOUTH

Ezekiel was a descendant of a priestly family, perhaps of the historic family of Zadok. To Ezekiel the Zadokites were the only legitimate priests. His turn of mind—by training and by natural endowment—clearly reveals the priest. In the year 597 B.C. he was led captive to Babylon; at what age we do not know. He was probably in his twenties. He settled with a group of fellow-exiles at Tel-Abib, a village in a rich, fertile valley, on the banks of the Chebar. This, it is believed, was a navigable canal intersecting a wide stretch of land between the Tigris and Euphrates rivers, southeast of the city of Babylon. Here, for twenty-two years, he served as "watchman"

[7] 34:6.   [8] 34:4–5.

over his people. We read of the prophet's "house" and of "elders" assembling in his home in the first few years of his settlement in Babylon. He seems to have been married at this time.[9]

We do know the spiritual climate of his youth. To what extent did it shape his mind and direct his spirit? He was probably a child when the frenzy of the Deuteronomic reformation swept Judah in the year 621. A wave of mourning swept the land upon the death of King Josiah in 608. The exile of Jehoahaz to Egypt and of Jehoiachim to Babylon was part of a major national disruption. This formed a landmark in the life of the young priest. One of the striking elegies in his book mourns this national tragedy.[10]

Jeremiah was an old man and a center of contention when Ezekiel was a young man. For thirty years prior to Ezekiel's captivity, Jeremiah had been a turbulent figure, preaching to crowds, cursing kings, attacking the priesthood. Nahum, Zephaniah, and Habakkuk were preaching the word of God with enraged eloquence. Did Ezekiel hear them or know them? Did reports of their activities come to him? We do not know. But scholars see strong kinship between Ezekiel and Jeremiah at many points. Echoes of Hosea's and Isaiah's oracles are discernible in his writings.

HIS BOOK

Most prominent in his book is his priestly background. He is alive to ritualistic offenses; his visions are in the form of Temple symbolism; his conception of Israel is

[9]3:24; 12:3 ff; 8:1; 19:1; 20:1; 24:18.   [10]Ezek. 19:1-9.

that of a congregation held together by ritual; his dream
for his people is that Israel shall be restored as a faithful
congregation worthy of their God. He is essentially a
Deuteronomist in the program he advances for his people.

Unlike his colleagues, Ezekiel was a literary man. The
call to prophecy, as we have seen it, was a call to swallow
a book, and he did it, he tells us.[11] "He exalted the book
phase of religion as no other prophet had done."[12] He
wrote his prophecies; then collected and edited them.
His aim, however, was practical rather than literary. Like
all the prophets, he directed his words—written or spoken
—at a definite goal. The text of his book is badly dam-
aged. This, combined with his extravagant imagery and
unearthly symbolism, makes it a difficult book. He is gar-
rulous and repetitious. This has been adduced as evidence
that he wrote his book in old age. He never wearies of
certain pet phrases. "The mountains of Israel," "house of
rebelliousness," "behold I am against . . . ," "I the Lord
have spoken of it" are forever on his tongue. The phrase
"son of man" occurs nearly a hundred times in his book.
His metaphors are profuse and badly tangled. But his
book abounds, too, in strong, vivid passages of singular
beauty. There is a wild dash of poetry in it, especially
the elegy. On the whole, however, Ezekiel's utterances are
more prosaic than those of the earlier prophets.

The chief difficulty of his book is the confusion between
the real and the imaginary, between fact and fancy.
Ezekiel saw all things in terms of certain moral realities.
The world before him and the life about him were only

[11]2:9—3:5.
[12]J. M. Powis Smith, *The Prophets and Their Times*, p. 175.

manifestations of a larger reality. He was captivated by the unearthly power. In it he lived and thought. What he experienced in fantasy and what he knew in life were often confused. Subject to trances, his ecstatic mind carried him beyond all bounds. Much of what he reports as fact can be explained only on the recognition that the prophet was subject to trances.[13]

His book is exceptional in several ways. It is far more systematic than any other prophetic book. The prophecies, on the whole, are chronologically arranged. They were reduced to writing by the prophet himself. He was probably far advanced in years when he gave final form to his writings.

The book of Ezekiel falls naturally into three parts:

a. 1–24, prophecies against Judah spoken before the fall of Judah in the year 586 B.C.

b. 25–32, oracles against the nations, spoken, for the most part, between the years 588 and 586 B.C.

c. 33–48, promises for the future, spoken between 585 and 573 B.C.

From the standpoint of literary style, the book of Ezekiel is one gorgeous tangle of symbolism. Symbolical visions and actions abound in wild profusion, often confusion. The prophet's habit of depicting his symbols in detail often obscures the brilliancy of conception. The imagery is always daring, always powerful. One or two instances will serve our purpose at this point by way of illustration.

[13]2:9—3:5, 15, 26; 4, etc. See G. A. Cooke, *ICC, Book of Ezekiel,* Introduction; A. B. Davidson, *CB, Ezekiel,* Introduction; J. M. Powis Smith, *The Prophets and Their Times,* Chap. X.

Judah is a lioness rearing her whelps into tearing young lions, only to be trapped and led into humiliating captivity; or Judah is a vine—an exuberant vine bursting with life by water courses—her branches climbing heavenward majestically, like ruler's sceptres, only to be plucked up, trampled upon, and withered under a scorching east wind. Egypt is a crocodile, fouling the water in his restless energy. Nebuchadrezzar is a giant speckled eagle with enormous pinions, a swooping menace. Image follows image in swift and gorgeous procession. We shall view some of them at closer range as we advance in our study of Ezekiel.

SYMBOLS AND ACTIONS

The facts of his life and the excitements of his mind are so closely interwoven that it is impossible to disentangle one from the other. What he saw and heard, what he spoke and did may or may not be taken as actual performances. Some of the fantastic actions he describes in intimate detail he probably did perform. We have observed other prophets behave in extraordinary manner. Hosea married an adultress by way of impressing a lesson on the minds of his people. Isaiah walked the streets of Jerusalm barefoot and naked for three years. That was his way of conveying a conviction to the lazy souls of Judah. Jeremiah clamped a wooden yoke around his neck and walked among his fellows in awkward posture to emphasize the burden that was on his heart. The Hebrew prophets were unusual men and did highly unusual things. They must not be judged by the standards of the average conventional person of our own time. Quite probably,

Ezekiel did perform some of the strange actions he reports. Some of them, no doubt, issued from his agitated imagination.

In his inaugural vision we see him swallowing a scroll, and, despite its lamentations, finding it sweet. He is carried to Tel Abib in the heat of spirit, while the hand of the Lord rests upon him. He remains dazed for seven days.[14] He is carried to Jerusalem by a lock of his head. There he explores the Temple and its environs, and gives us a detailed description of the idolatry to which Jerusalem had abandoned herself—idols without and within the Temple, women lamenting for Tammuz, the Babylonian god of fertility, men worshipping the sun.[15] He draws a sketch of Jerusalem on a brick and enacts before the wondering observers the siege and fall of the Holy City.[16] He lies on his left side three hundred and ninety days and on his right side forty days. These days represented as many years in the history of Israel and Judah. Thus does he "bear the iniquity" of his nation. As he is helpless under his burden, so are Israel and Judah helpless under the burden of their sins.[17] He prepares revolting food and eats it sparingly, thus testifying to the slow starvation and pollution that shall come upon Jerusalem.[18] Using a barber's razor, he shaves off the hair of his head and beard, weighs it into three equal parts and destroys each part separately. Thus shall Jerusalem be shorn and her children destroyed.[19] He lumps into a bundle his ragged belongings and in frenzied haste breaks through a wall of his house, as if escaping from a besieged city. Thus shall be the fate of those who dwell in Jerusalem.

[14] 2:9—3:2.   [15] 8.   [16] 4:1-3   [17] 4:4-8.   [18] 4:9-17.   [19] 5:1-4.

He eats bread and drinks water in violent haste, trembling with agitation, thus giving further testimony of the fate that shall befall Jerusalem.[20] He beats himself violently, for he sees a glittering sword hanging over his people.[21]

His wife died nine years after he settled in Babylon. That, too, becomes a symbol and an omen.

Also the word of the Lord came unto me, saying: "Son of man, behold, I take away from thee the desire of thine eyes with a stroke; yet neither shalt thou make lamentation nor weep, neither shall thy tears run down. Sigh in silence; make no mourning for the dead, bind thy headtire upon thee, and put thy shoes upon thy feet, and cover not thine upper lip, and eat not the bread of man." So I spoke unto the people in the morning, and at even my wife died; and I did in the morning as I was commanded.[22]

Thus shall the sanctuary, the pride and joy of the people, be no more, but there shall be no mourning, for all hearts shall be numbed and all eyes dry of tears.

These are some of the more striking symbolic actions reported in the book of Ezekiel. Some he no doubt performed; others can be understood only on the basis of ecstasy. Maimonides observes: "It was in a prophetic vision that he did all these actions which he was commanded to do. . . . Weak-minded persons believe that the prophet relates here what he was commanded to do, and what he actually did . . . but it is distinctly stated that all this took place in a vision."[23] Maimonides rationalizes too much.

[20]12:3–7, 17–20.   [21]21:9–15.   [22]24:15–18.
[23]*Guide for the Perplexed*, ed. Friedlander, p. 246.

HIS PERSONALITY

An engaging and baffling personality stands revealed in the book of Ezekiel. A bundle of contradictions, he is nevertheless a consistent personality.

Clearly pathologic, he is, nevertheless, systematic and logical. His book follows an orderly pattern. He formulates a coherent system of faith and ritual and evolves a system of legislation. Intensively imaginative and speaking in a profusion of metaphors, he is, at the same time, prosaic and wordy. His love of detail turns some of his brilliant conceptions into dull expositions.

He is priest and prophet in one. The prophetic motivated the priestly, and the priestly stabilized the prophetic. Prophet, he is nonetheless fond of the pomp of priesthood. His conception of God made him a universalist, after the manner of his prophetic tradition; his particularistic view of his people made him a nationalist. As Professor Lods expresses it, to the mind of Ezekiel "Israel was the chosen people of the universal God."[24] But loving Israel though he did, he brands it as a degraded people. Other prophets denouncing Israel saw it as a noble people in its youth. Ezekiel condemns it as a corrupt people from its very beginnings.[25] Nevertheless, he sees in these very people the only hope for the restoration and regeneration of Judah. Strictly monotheistic, he, at he same time, absorbed much of the impressions of Babylonian polytheism.[26] He is a rigid moralist. The doubts that beset Jeremiah, the tender compassion that distinguished Hosea,

[24]*The Prophets and the Rise of Judaism*, p. 231.
[25]16.   [26]Lods, *ibid.*, p. 230.

are absent in Ezekiel. He is more like Amos in his dogmatic severity. The "rebellious house" must be destroyed
by the sword and the Temple must perish so that God's
"honor" may be vindicated and His "glory" restored.
When Jerusalem fell, not a word of pity dropped from
his severe lips. Nevertheless, the same Ezekiel proclaims
that the just shall not die for the sins of the wicked,
that repentance saves and redeems, and that God's desire
is that sin and not the sinner shall perish. And the burden
of all his preachments is to restore life and faith.

He shares in full measure the moral strength and unbending rectitude of the prophets. His teachings were
apparently spurned by his fellows. The same people, however, were drawn to him. He knew the fate of the popular
preacher; people came merely to listen to his voice. They
hear his words but

lo, thou art unto them as a love song of one that hath a
pleasant voice, and can play well on an instrument; so
they hear thy words, but they do them not.[27]

Nevertheless, the people will know that a prophet was in
their midst.

THE BURDEN OF HIS SOUL

Prior to the year 586 B.C. Ezekiel's preachments reduced themselves to one tragic conviction: Jerusalem must
fall. This was the great burden that rested upon his
soul, and to this he gave constant emphasis, often in
grotesque terms. Why such a fate for Judah and Jerusalem? Because the nation had sinned. His condemnation of

[27] 33:32.

Judah was even more violent than that of his prophetic predecessors. Israel is a corrupt, hybrid people:

Thine origin and thy nativity is of the land of the Canaanite; the Ammorite was thy father, and thy mother was a Hittite.[28]

From her youth onward Israel was the child of wild passion, and she grew into a promiscuous prostitute. Hosea, employing the same metaphor, had spoken tenderly and made it yield a lesson in compassion; in the mouth of Ezekiel the metaphor is a ferocious stricture. Isaiah had compared Judah to a vineyard that proved to be a disappointment; others had spoken of Israel as "the vine of His planting." Ezekiel accepted the metaphor but gave it new emphasis: the vine is a creeping, weak, helpless thing in the forest, especially "when the fire had devoured it and it is singed."

Therefore thus saith the Lord God: As the vinetree among the trees of the forest, which I have given to the fire for fuel, so do I give the inhabitants of Jerusalem. And I will set My face against them; out of the fire are they come forth, and the fire shall devour them; and ye shall know that I am the Lord, when I set My face against them. And I will make the land desolate, because they have acted treacherously, saith the Lord God.[29]

Why so much emphasis upon the wickedness of Jerusalem and why such endless repetition of the sad news that the city must fall? Because God is just. If punishment falls upon Judah, it is because Judah has sinned, sinned abominably. Thus the prophet sought to vindicate the justice of God.

[28]16:3.   [29]15:6–8.

But God is also merciful and forgiving. Ezekiel did not lose this conviction entirely. Hope and mercy never abandoned him. Purged of its rebels and idolators, Israel shall be restored to its holy mountain and shall once again enter His courts with "sweet savour." Before many years had passed, Ezekiel came to emphasize this "merciful and gracious" attribute of God, but before the fall of the Temple it was subordinated to his message of doom.

After 586 B.C. the tone and content of his message changed. Once his prophecy was fulfilled and Jerusalem lay in ashes, her children dead, abandoned or exiled, the prophet could no longer repeat his sad refrain. Now it was a time for comfort. Broken hearts and torn minds were everywhere. Doubts haunted sensitive men. The good and the bad were alike crushed in the same mass disaster. If God were just, why did He permit such indiscriminate suffering? And was this particular generation worse than earlier ones? Moreover, now that they were caught in this cruel scheme, how might they hope to extricate themselves? How live? Despair hung over all. God Himself had abandoned them. "Our transgressions and our sins are upon us, and we pine away in them; how then shall we live?"[30]

The times called for reconstruction in the religious life of Judah. Ezekiel took his place as the prophet of reconstruction. It was an enormous task. It required a daring rebuilding of the life and faith of Israel. From the spiritual necessity of his day issued his central teaching and his special contribution to the faith of Israel.

Two basic principles guided Ezekiel in the reconstruc-

[30]33:10. See Chap. X of present work.

tion of the religious thought of Israel. One was the freedom and the responsibility of the individual; the other,
the efficacy of repentance. Neither of these was original
to him; both had been developing and gaining in emphasis. Among the prophets, Jeremiah especially had felt
his way toward these; among the legislators, the Deu-
teronomists had given expression to them. Ezekiel, however, gave them clear and energetic form. Henceforth
they became doctrines in the religion of Israel.

In a chapter that has become classic in the theologic
thought of Judaism and Christianity,[31] Ezekiel develops
his thought:

And the word of the Lord came unto me, saying: What
mean ye, that ye use this proverb in the land of Israel,
saying:

> The Fathers have eaten sour grapes,
> And the children's teeth are set on edge?

As I live, saith the Lord God, ye shall not have occasion
any more to use this proverb in Israel. Behold, all souls
are Mine; as the soul of the father, so also the soul of
the son is Mine; the soul that sinneth, it shall die.[32]

The proverb Ezekiel repudiates must have been on the
tongues of men. It was no doubt spoken by men of varied
mood. Some spoke it cynically, some in despair, some in
self-righteousness. But whatever the mood in which it
was uttered, it testified to the low ebb of the religious life
among the exiles. Ezekiel rejects the current wisdom and
proclaims as divine truth the principle that "the soul
that sinneth it shall die"; *it* and none other. Jeremiah
had hoped for the ideal day when no man would suffer

[31]18. See also 3:16–21; 23:12–20.   [32]18:1–4.

for the sins of another.[33] What was only a hope to Jeremiah was an established truth to Ezekiel.

In characteristic manner Ezekiel develops the thought in detail. The righteous man shall live by virtue of his righteousness. If he have a wicked son, that wicked son shall perish because of his wickedness. The righteousness of his father shall not avail him. If this wicked son have a son and he be righteous, he shall live. The sins of the fathers shall not be visited upon the children.

Every man is free to be righteous and live or to be wicked and perish. But what of him who has sinned? Is he doomed forever? Here Ezekiel advances his second principle. The sinner who repents shall live. Repentance brings God's forgiveness, for what God desires is not the death of the sinner but that "he return and live." Thus the individual soul may free itself not only from the evil heritage of the fathers but from the ban of its own past as well.

How might the Judean exiles by the waters of Babylon live? Were they a doomed, lost generation? How might they reorganize their lives? By embracing fully the truth that every man is a free moral agent, responsible to God for his own acts, and by repenting of the evil. Thus Ezekiel pleads:

Cast away from you all your transgressions, wherein ye have transgressed; and make you a new heart and a new spirit; for why will ye die, O house of Israel? For I have no pleasure in the death of him that dieth, saith the Lord God; wherefore turn yourselves, and live.[34]

[33]Jer. 21:29.
[34]18:31–32. See J. M. Powis Smith, *The Prophet and His Problems*, Chap. VII.

It should be noted that Ezekiel is thinking in terms of the individual, not the nation. The nation was gone; the individual remained. In this shift from the group to the individual—and in this insistence that the individual is a free and responsible moral agent before God, determining his own fate by his own conduct—Ezekiel made his chief contribution to the religious thought of mankind.

The doctrine is vulnerable, of course. Obviously, Ezekiel overstates his case. It may be argued that it is not true to the realities of life. It would be much closer to the facts to say that the sins of the fathers plague the children unto the second, third, and fourth generations. Biologically and sociologically this would be a truer observation. It may be stated, too, that a man cannot shake off his evil past so easily as Ezekiel assumes. Nevertheless, by insisting upon the freedom and the responsibility of the individual, Ezekiel gives us the groundwork of our ethics and all moral living. Moreover, as Montefiore observes, "It was a step of enormous value in the direction of personal religion, and towards a better theory of the relation of man to God. . . . Ezekiel broke forever with the false notion of divine vengeance transmitted from generation to generation, and from the equally false and despairing idea that repentance is beyond human power."[35]

IN THE VALLEY OF DRY BONES

In shifting from the nation to the individual, Ezekiel had no thought of preaching an individualistic type of religion. His aim was to regenerate the nation by re-

[35]Claude G. Montefiore, *Hibbert Lectures* (1897), p. 253.

habilitating the moral life of the individual. In time the nation would arise reborn and reconsecrated by the sheer power of the righteous men who would make up its citizenry.

The rebirth of the nation is stated in one of Ezekiel's most powerful visions. The hand of God rests upon him, and he finds himself in a broad valley filled with the bleached bones of men:

And He caused me to pass by them round about, and, behold, there were very many in the open valley; and lo, they were very dry. And He said unto me: "Son of man, can these bones live?" And I answered: "O Lord God, Thou knowest." Then He said unto me: "Prophesy over these bones, and say unto them: O ye dry bones, hear the word of the Lord: Thus saith the Lord God unto these bones: Behold, I will cause breath to enter into you, and ye shall live. And I will lay sinews upon you, and will bring up flesh upon you, and cover you with skin, and put breath in you, and ye shall live; and ye shall know that I am the Lord." So I prophesied as I was commanded; and as I prophesied, there was a noise, and behold a commotion, and the bones came together, bone to its bone. And I beheld, and, lo, there were sinews upon them, and flesh came up, and skin covered them above; but there was no breath in them. Then said He unto me: "Prophesy unto the breath, prophesy, son of man, and say to the breath: Thus saith the Lord God: Come from the four winds, O breath, and breathe upon these slain, that they may live." So I prophesied as He commanded me, and the breath came into them, and they lived, and stood up upon their feet, an exceeding great host.[36]

What this manifestation announces is clear. The spirit of God shall reanimate the dry bones of Judah. Thus

[36]37:2–10.

Ezekiel sought to dispel the despair that had settled over the minds of his fellow-exiles. Life, not death, is what God desires for His people.[37]

He repeats his lesson of national restoration and regeneration by a symbolic act, comprehensible to the dullest mind. He takes two sticks, writes on one, "For Judah," and upon the other, "For Ephraim," and ties the two sticks together. The divided nation shall become one. An ideal ruler, a scion of King David, will rule over the restored nation. An everlasting covenant shall bind God and Israel. It shall be a covenant of peace. Thus shall God come to dwell among His people and sanctify them.[38] The fact that the ten tribes of Israel had been carried off captive by Assyria some one hundred and forty years earlier and that the Babylonian conqueror of Judah showed no signs of weakening his grip did not disturb the prophet in his faith in God. The Shepherd will gather His scattered flock and lead them back to His holy mountain. Ezekiel lived by faith.

The nations that held Israel captive shall fall. They will collapse under the impact of God's will, as the earlier prophets had foretold. Not Israel but God will fight the battle. It will be a world-shaking war. The Kingdom of God will triumph over the forces of evil, and God alone will be exalted on that day. Here we have one of the apocalypses that are so common to Ezekiel.[39]

It must be noted that Ezekiel's vision of the restoration is not merely nationalistic. It does include a return to the soil of Israel; it does emphasize an independent nation

[37]To consider Ezekiel 37 as a divine promise of personal resurrection, as the chapter has been interpreted by various theologians, is inaccurate.
[38]37:15–38. [39]38–39.

under a descendant of Israel's most popular King, David. But all this is only the external form. Essentially it shall be a spiritual return, a return to holiness and God's will.

A new heart also will I give you, and a new spirit will I put within you; and I will take away the stony heart out of your flesh, and I will give you a heart of flesh. And I will put my spirit within you, and cause you to walk in My statutes, and ye shall keep Mine ordinances, and do them. And ye shall dwell in the land that I gave to your fathers; and ye shall be My people, and I will be your God.[40]

Jerusalem shall be reborn as a religious community; Israel shall flower not as a nation in the restricted political sense but as a congregation.

SILENCE AND FINAL VISIONS

Twelve years of silence follow Ezekiel's announcement of his vision of Israel's restoration. How to explain this silence is one of the problems facing the scholars. In the life of so fiery and articulate a personality twelve years of silence is a tremendous fact. Was it due to some physical handicap that sealed his lips? Was it due to some mental disturbance? Or is the silence due to an incomplete report of the prophet's life and speech?

Ezekiel's last visions and utterances belong to the year 573–572 B.C.[41] They are essentially a practical but highly inspired program for redeemed Israel on a transformed earth, under a benevolent heaven. It is a religious Utopia. The memories of his youth as priest in the Temple are

[40]36:26–28.   [41]40–48.

now transformed into the visions of his old age yearning for a new sanctuary.

In vision he is transported to the land of Israel and placed on a high mountain, from the heights of which he could see the Golden City of his dreams. An angel appears and presents himself as guide. The prophet is told to observe carefully so that he may teach his people accurately.

The heavenly guide points out the details in a grand structure that embodies all that the prophet had dreamed for his people. He observes the new Temple, pauses before the various courts, gates, altars. The Glory of God pours in by the eastern gateway, and He Himself consecrates His new shrine. Never again must it be profaned. The priestly hierarchy is defined; the duties, rights, and prerogatives of the priests and Levites are stated. In weary detail the ceremonial and sacrificial systems are described. Much of this is no doubt the elaboration of priestly scribes.[42]

From the Temple issues a tiny stream. A thousand feet from its source it is only ankle-deep. But rapidly it gains volume and power and turns into a mighty river as it descends into the Dead Sea. It turns the Dead Sea and its bitter waters into a fresh-water lake swarming with fish, and transforms the intervening wasteland into a luxuriant garden. This is the River of Life flowing from the heights of the Mountain of the Lord.[43]

All his dreams and visions, preachments and teachings thus culminate in a sanctuary. Israel is one congregation. It is a redeemed Israel. The vulgar shall not profane its

[42]See G. A. Cooke, *Book of Ezekiel, ICC,* Introduction.   [43]47:1–12.

soul nor desecrate its shrine. Over all shall rest the holy, for God shall be there.

We know nothing of his last years.

BUILDER OF JUDAISM

What were the final results of all the dreams, trances, exhortations, and particularistic legalism of this strange man? One positive gain, which has affected the moral life of mankind profoundly, is the emphasis upon the freedom and responsibility of the individual. Without it we can have no individual morality. All we can have are tribal taboos. A second gain is the reality of atonement. Sincere repentance breaks the chains that hold every man captive and gives him a new page whereon to write a new chapter of his life. The third gain that has come into our spiritual heritage is the impetus Ezekiel gave to the apocalyptic and eschatologic—those weird, fantastic yet fascinating revelations and speculations as to what will happen in the end of days. A rich, colorful, if bizarre, literature was inspired largely by Ezekiel's visions. Much of it became authoritative in Judaism and Christianity. Many a controversy in the history of the Synagogue and Church alike may be traced to one vision or another in the book of Ezekiel.

To Israel especially, scattered over the face of the earth and across the centuries, Ezekiel left a double heritage, a heritage by which Israel is distinguished and preserved. One is the conviction that Israel spells one congregation, held together by religious traditions and forms. This lifts Israel above the tribal nationalism and vicious racialism of our own time. The other is his fusion of law and prophecy into *Torah*, thereby channelling and giving authoritative form to the life of religious Israel.

The earlier prophets we have been considering had denounced the religious practices of their times, but they did not advance an alternative system. In Deuteronomy the effort is made to combine the priestly with the prophetic. Ezekiel carries this farther. He makes law and prophecy interdependent. The moral fire which characterizes prophecy and the discipline which distinguishes the religion of the priests merged into a new synthesis: *Torah*. Henceforth prophecy and law became abiding elements in the religion of Israel. Prophecy saved Judaism from degenerating into smug ecclesiasticism; the law saved it from the fate of futile flashes of lightning in the night.

The legislative structure Ezekiel rears in the last chapters of his book became the impetus to much legislative effort. The leaders of the torn community sought to unite and safeguard it by evolving a religious system in terms of law and moral principles as taught in their Hebraic traditions by priests and prophets. In the course of time came scribes, sages, and rabbis and continued building the system of faith and life. Henceforth it was not law alone and not prophecy alone; henceforth it was *Torah*.

Thus Ezekiel "formed the plan and shaped the ideals on which later Judaism was built. . . . All that has been persistent and fundamental in the Judaism of twenty centuries can be traced back to Ezekiel."[44]

[44]W. F. Lofthouse, *The Prophet of Reconstruction* (1920), p. 20.

XII

DEUTERO–ISAIAH

Comfort ye, comfort ye my people, saith the Lord. . . .

For the mountains may depart
And the hills be removed;
But my kindness shall not depart from thee,
Neither shall My covenant of peace be removed,
Saith the Lord that hath compassion on thee.

ISAIAH 40:1; 54:10.

CYRUS

WHILE Ezekiel was watching over the household of Israel in exile and dreaming heroic plans for its restoration, the path of empire was shifting again. Once more Israel was at a sharp turn in its destiny.

In the northwest corner of Elam, a dependency of Media, a powerful personality arose. His relentless armies filled the world with alarm. His name was Cyrus. By descent he was a Persian; by religion a Zoroastrian. In 558 B.C. he usurped the throne of Ansham. Within ten years he established the far-flung Medo-Persian Empire from the River Indus in the east to the Ægean Sea in the west. He clamped his power on Media, Persia, northern Babylon, Armenia, Asia Minor, and all the Greek provinces as far as the Hellespont. In his path lay Babylon, once vigorous, now senile, mistress of the world. Would his armies, thus far invincible, master Babylon?

175

Echoes of the exploits of Cyrus reverberated throughout Babylon and agitated the minds of the homesick exiles with renewed hopes of liberation. Cyrus not only conquered province after province but set captive peoples free and made due obeisance to their gods. Plainly God was mindful of His own; promises made by His prophets were being fulfilled. Redemption was on the march; salvation was on the wing. The hour of doom for Babylon had struck. Poets caught the vision and gave expression to their hopes in vigorous rhythm.[1] One unknown poet chanted a sarcastic elegy over the fallen King of Babylon. His fate was sealed in the mind of God:

> The nether-world from beneath is moved for thee
> To meet thee at thy coming;
> The shades are stirred up for thee,
> Even all the chief ones of the earth;
> All the kings of the nations
> Are raised up from their thrones.
> All they do answer
> And say unto thee:
> "Art thou also become weak as we?
> Art thou become like unto us?
> Thy pomp is brought down to the nether-world,
> And the noise of thy psalteries;
> The maggot is spread under thee,
> And the worms cover thee."
>
> How art thou fallen from heaven,
> O day-star, son of the morning!
> How art thou cut down to the ground,
> That didst cast lots over the nations!
> And thou saidst in thy heart:

[1] Isa. 13–14; 21.

"I will ascend into heaven,
Above the stars of God
Will I exalt my throne;
And I will sit upon the mount of meeting,
In the uttermost parts of the north;
I will ascend above the heights of the clouds;
I will be like the Most High."
Yet thou shalt be brought down to the nether-world,
To the uttermost parts of the pit.[2]

One of these unknown poets who sensed imminent redemption for the Judean captives and gave expression to his conviction in enchanting, haunting words is known to us by the prosaic name of "Deutero-Isaiah," or "the Second Isaiah." In rapturous, contagious enthusiasm he hailed Cyrus as the anointed of the Lord, one sent by the Holy One of Israel to set His people free. Who this prophet-poet was we do not know. Not a single fact in the story of his life has come down to us. He is supposed to have lived, according to various scholars, in Babylon, Elam, Phœnicia, Egypt, Ethiopia, Sheba, Western Asia, and Palestine. Even his name is not recorded in history. His magnificent songs and prophecies, however—some, if not all—have been preserved as part of the book of Isaiah. They represent the high-water mark in the prophecy and poetry of Israel.

ISAIAH 40–66

Critical students of the Bible are agreed that the last twenty-seven chapters of the book of Isaiah are not the writings of the prophet Isaiah. They belong to a later age. Three lines of evidence drawn from these chapters

[2]Isa. 14:9–15.

offer convincing proof. *First,* the political conditions re-
flected in these poems do not belong to the age of Isaiah
(740–701). Cyrus is hailed repeatedly; twice he is mentioned by name. There are some one hundred and fifty or
sixty years between Cyrus and the prophet Isaiah. The
situation contemplated in chapters 40–55 is clearly the
Babylonian exile; the last ten chapters reflect an even
later age. *Secondly,* the characteristic conceptions and
points of emphasis of these twenty-seven chapters mark
them off from the preceding thirty-nine of the book of
Isaiah. Isaiah's thought of an elect remnant is barely mentioned in 40–66, while the mission of Israel, propounded
with much force in the last chapters, is not mentioned
in the previous portion of the book. Other evidence might
be cited, such as the nature of the description of God.
Thirdly, the two parts of the book of Isaiah vary strikingly in their literary characteristics. Deutero-Isaiah is
profuse, lyrical, given to repetition and argumentation
while Isaiah is terse, often abrupt, hardly ever repeating
himself.

Scholars are further agreed that these twenty-seven
chapters are not the work of one author and that they
do not belong to one age. This, too, has been well established by evidence drawn from the text.

Logically the chapters fall into three groups: *A,* 40–48;
B, 49–55; *C,* 56–66. The general agreement among the
critical scholars is that groups *A* and *B* are the work of
one author. Because these chapters hail the advent of
Cyrus, extol his victories over many nations and antici-
pate his conquest of Babylon, scholars place them between the years 546 B.C., when Cyrus scored his great

victory over Lydia and captivated the imaginations of men as a world conqueror, and 538 B.C., when Babylon finally surrendered to him. Section *C*, the same scholars maintain, belongs to a later age. Its atmosphere is Palestinian. The social conditions this section reflects are those known to have existed in the period of Ezra-Nehemiah. Thus some three quarters of a century separates chapters 56–66 from 40–55.[3] The unknown author (or authors) of these chapters is usually spoken of as Trito-Isaiah.

RELIGIOUS CONCEPTIONS OF DEUTERO-ISAIAH

Deutero-Isaiah is symphonic in thought and in literary expression. He strikes with might and charm on all the instruments known to the inspired poet. Certain themes dominate his thinking; he reverts to them again and again. Minor themes swell the chorus, blend and fade with the surging rhythm. The major themes may be reduced to three.

First is the glad tidings that Israel shall be redeemed with an everlasting salvation. God has raised up a redeemer in the person of Cyrus. He shall subjugate Babylon and set the Judean captives free. This is the central theme in the poems of Deutero-Isaiah, the sweet burden of his soul.

The *second* major theme is the grandeur of God. Deutero-Isaiah gives classic expression to the conception of ethical monotheism. Earlier prophets assumed or implied this same view of God and the universe, but it was left to Deutero-Isaiah to state it in majestic terms as an abstract

[3]For a detailed discussion, see J. Skinner. *CB*, to Isaiah 40–66, Introduction.

truth of religion. God is incomparable; His purposes cannot be thwarted by men. Nature and history throb with His august presence. "I am God and there is none else." "Before Me there was no God formed, neither shall there be after Me." He is "First and Last," who called all the generations into being. Righteous, trustworthy, compassionate, He is a living God whose presence fills the world.

The reverse of this conception is the notion of the idol. Because God is holy and incomprehensible, the puny little idol is ridiculous. It is not so much the sin of idolatry as its stupidity that draws the biting sarcasm of Deutero-Isaiah.

The *third* theme controlling the poems of Deutero-Isaiah is the conception of Israel as the Servant of the Lord. Israel is the elect servant of God. From its earliest beginnings Israel has been drafted by God to champion His truth in the world. This is the meaning of Israel's life. Thus is Israel charged with a mission. This mission is to bring light to blind eyes, to establish truth, justice and mercy in the world. Israel, by its life and worship, must redeem mankind of its idolatries.

We turn to the prophet's own words for the truths he speaks, for who may hope to approximate the grandeur of his speech? As we read his lines, let us note the surge of music that permeates them even in translation, the wealth of imagery and, above all, the tenderness of his words.

PRELUDE: DIVINE COMFORT TO A STRICKEN PEOPLE

Enraptured with a new-born hope, the prophet-poet announces glad news: Zion shall be restored! Israel is redeemed! God has forgiven and Israel is delivered. Let Israel therefore be comforted. "Behold your God!"

> Comfort ye, comfort ye my people,
> Saith your God.
> Speak ye to the heart of Jerusalem,
> And cry unto her,
> That her time of service is accomplished,
> That her guilt is paid off;
> That she hath received at the Lord's hand
> Double for all her sins.[4]

A voice is heard calling on unseen powers to prepare the way of the Lord. All nature is rocked by the pounding feet of the marching destiny of Israel. All earthly power is transitory; only the word of God is eternal, and He is returning to His own.

> Hark! one calleth:
> "Clear ye in the wilderness the way of the Lord,
> Make straight in the desert
> A highway for our God.
> Every valley shall be lifted up,
> And every mountain and hill shall be made low;
> And the rugged shall be made level,
> And the rough places a plain;
> And the glory of the Lord shall be revealed,
> And all the flesh shall see it together;
> For the mouth of the Lord hath spoken it."[5]

> Hark! one saith, "Proclaim!"
> And I said, "What shall I proclaim?"
> "All flesh is grass,
> And the goodliness thereof is as the flower
>   of the field;

440:1–2.   [5]40:3–5.

The grass withereth, the flower fadeth;
Because the breath of the Lord bloweth upon it.
Surely the people is grass.
The grass withereth, the flower fadeth;
But the word of our God shall stand forever."[6]

O thou that tellest good tidings to Zion,
Get thee up into the high mountain;
O thou that tellest good tidings to Jerusalem,
Lift up thy voice with strength;
Lift it up, be not afraid;
Say unto the cities of Judah:
"Behold your God!"
Behold, the Lord God will come as a Mighty One,
And His arm will rule for Him;
Behold, His reward is with Him
And His recompense before Him.
He shall feed His flock like a shepherd,
He shall gather the lambs in His arm,
And carry them in His bosom,
And shall gently lead those that give suck.[7]

In a magnificent passage, the might and grandeur of
God are recalled to reassure the discouraged people. The
folly of worshipping a dumb idol in view of this grandeur
draws the contempt of the prophet.

Who hath measured the waters in the hollow of his hand,
And meted out heaven with the span
And comprehended the dust of the earth in a measure,
And weighed the mountains in scales,
And the hills in a balance?
Who hath directed the spirit of the Lord,
Or who was His counsellor that he might instruct Him?
With whom took He counsel, and who instructed Him,

[6] 40:6-8.   [7] 40:9-11.

And taught Him knowledge,
And made Him to know the way of discernment?
Behold, the nations are as a drop of a bucket,
And are counted as the small dust of the balance.
Behold, the isles are as a mote in weight.
And Lebanon is not sufficient fuel,
Nor the beasts thereof sufficient for burnt-offerings.
All the nations are as nothing before Him;
They are accounted by Him as things of nought,
    and vanity.

To whom then will ye liken God?
Or what likeness will ye compare unto Him?
The image perchance, which the craftsman hath melted,
And the goldsmith spread over with gold,
The silversmith casting silver chains?
A holm-oak is set apart,
He chooseth a tree that will not rot;
He seeketh unto him a cunning craftsman
To set up an image, that shall not be moved.

Know ye not? Hear ye not?
Hath it not been told you from the beginning?
Have ye not understood the foundations of the earth?
It is He that sitteth above the circle of the earth,
And the inhabitants thereof are as grasshoppers;
That stretcheth out the heavens as a curtain,
And spreadeth them out as a tent to dwell in;
That bringeth princes to nothing;
And maketh the judges of the earth as a thing
    of nought.
Scarce are they planted,
Scarce are they sown,
Scarce hath their stock taken root in the earth;
When he bloweth upon them, they wither,
And the whirlwind taketh them away as stubble.

To whom then will ye liken Me, that I should be equal?
Saith the Holy One.
Lift up your eyes on high
And see: Who hath created these?
He that bringeth out their host by number,
He calleth them all by name;
Before One so great in might and strong in power—
Not one is missing.[8]

The world and human destiny being in the hands of
so majestic a Power, there is abundant reason for faith
and hope for Israel. "He giveth power to the faint."

Why sayest thou, O Jacob,
And speakest, O Israel:
"My way is hid from the Lord,
And my right is passed over from my God"?
Hast thou not known? hast thou not heard
That the everlasting God, the Lord,
The Creator of the ends of the earth,
Fainteth not, neither is weary?
His discernment is past searching out.
He giveth power to the faint;
And to him that hath no might He increaseth strength.

Even the youths shall faint and be weary,
And the young men shall utterly fall;
But they that wait for the Lord
    shall renew their strength;
They shall mount up with wings as eagles;
They shall run, and not be weary;
They shall walk, and not faint.[9]

REDEMPTION IS NIGH

God has not cast off His own. From the standpoint of
the eternal, His anger is but for a moment; His mercies

[8] 40:12-26.   [9] 40:27-31.

reach unto all generations. He will ransom His people at the cost of the arrogant and cruel powers of the earth. Wedded to God, the scattered children of Israel will be gathered together and form one invincible community.

But now thus saith the Lord that created thee,
    O Jacob,
And He that formed thee, O Israel:
Fear not, for I have redeemed thee,
I have called thee by thy name, thou art Mine.
When thou passest through the waters,
    I will be with thee,
And through the rivers, they shall not overflow thee;
When thou walkest through the fire,
    thou shalt not be burned,
Neither shall the flame kindle upon thee.
For I am the Lord thy God,
The Holy One of Israel, thy Saviour,
I have given Egypt as thy ransom,
Ethiopia and Seba for thee.
Since thou art precious in My sight,
    and honourable,
And I have loved thee;
Therefore will I give men for thee,
And peoples for thy life.
Fear not, for I am with thee;
I will bring thy seed from the east,
    and gather thee from the west;
I will say to the north: "Give up,"
And to the south: "Keep not back,
Bring My sons from far,
And My daughters from the end of the earth;
Every one that is called by My name,
And whom I have created for My glory,
I have formed him, yea, I have made him."[10]
[10]43:1-7.

Let Israel return to God in joyous faith; let heaven and earth sing for joy.

> I have blotted out, as a thick cloud,
>   thy transgressions,
> And, as a cloud, thy sins;
> Return unto Me, for I have redeemed thee.
> Sing, O ye heavens, for the Lord hath done it;
> Shout, ye lowest parts of the earth;
> Break forth into singing, ye mountains,
> O forest, and every tree therein;
> For the Lord hath redeemed Jacob,
> And doth glorify Himself in Israel.[11]

Again the poet seeks to rouse the weary spirit of Israel with the assurance of God's eternal love.

> But Zion said: "The Lord hath forsaken me,
> And the Lord hath forgotten me."
> Can a woman forget her sucking child,
> That she should not have compassion
>   on the son of her womb?
> Yea, these may forget,
> Yet will not I forget thee.[12]

Why fear the reproaches of men when God is everlasting and merciful?

> Lift up your eyes to the heavens,
> And look upon the earth beneath;
> For the heavens shall vanish away like smoke,
> And the earth shall wax old like a garment,
> And they that dwell therein shall die
>   in like manner;
> But My salvation shall be for ever,
> And My favour shall not be abolished.

Hearken unto Me, ye that know righteousness,

[11] 44:22-23.   [12] 49:14-15.

The people in whose heart is My law;
Fear ye not the taunt of men,
Neither be ye dismayed at their revilings.
For the moth shall eat them up like a garment,
And the worm shall eat them like wool;
But My favour shall be for ever,
And My salvation unto all generations.

Awake, awake, put on strength,
O arm of the Lord;
Awake, as in the days of old,
The generations of ancient times.

.   .   .   .

And the ransomed of the Lord shall return,
And come with singing unto Zion,
And everlasting joy shall be upon their heads;
They shall obtain gladness and joy,
And sorrow and sighing shall flee away.

.   .   .   .

Awake, awake,
Stand up, O Jerusalem,
That hast drunken the beaker,
      even the cup of staggering,
And drained it.[13]

Heralds of the good news are on the way; they are coming up the holy mountain. The watchmen on the city walls pick up the news and swell the chorus, rousing the dejected people from their stupor.

How beautiful upon the mountains
Are the feet of the messenger of
      good tidings,

[13]51:6–9a, 11, 17.

That announceth peace, the harbinger
    of good tidings,
That announceth salvation;
That saith unto Zion:
"Thy God reigneth!"
Hark, thy watchmen! they lift up
    the voice,
Together do they sing;
For they shall see, eye to eye,
The Lord returning to Zion.
Break forth into joy, sing together,
Ye waste places of Jerusalem;
For the Lord hath comforted His people,
He hath redeemed Jerusalem.[14]

CYRUS, GOD'S ANOINTED

Beloved of the gods was Cyrus. Nation after nation surrendered to him; shrine after shrine received and blessed him. A Babylonian historian describes him as the favorite of Marduk. Deutero-Isaiah hails him as God's friend, God's anointed. He is the chosen agent fulfilling His will. He shall liberate Israel.

Thus saith the Lord of His anointed,
To Cyrus, whose right hand I have holden,
To subdue nations before him,
And to loose the loins of kings;
To open the doors before him,
And that the gates may not be shut:
I will go before thee,
And make the crooked places straight;
I will break in pieces the doors of brass,
And cut in sunder the bars of iron;
And I will give thee the treasures of darkness,

[14]52:7–9.

And hidden riches of secret places,
That thou mayest know that I am the Lord,
Who call thee by thy name, even the God of Israel.
For the sake of Jacob My servant,
And Israel Mine elect,
I have called thee by thy name,
I have surnamed thee, though thou hast not
    known Me.
I am the Lord, and there is none else,
Beside Me there is no God;

I have girded thee, though thou
    hast not known Me;
That they may know from the rising
    of the sun, and from the west,
That there is none beside Me;
I am the Lord, and there is none else;
I form the light, and create darkness;
I make peace, and create evil;
I am the Lord, that doeth all these things.

Drop down, ye heavens, from above,
And let the skies pour down righteousness;
Let the earth open, that they may bring
    forth salvation,
And let her cause righteousness
    to spring up together;
I the Lord have created it.[15]

GOD, SOVEREIGN AND ETERNAL

In the Prelude we have read one of Deutero-Isaiah's
hymns extolling the sovereignty of God.[16] Nature and
history reveal His majesty. The poet reverts to this theme
repeatedly. If Cyrus brings deliverance, it is only external,

[15]45:1–8. See also 41:2–4.   [16]40:12–41.

and he is only the unconscious agent of His will. Shall the
handle of the axe boast itself against him that swings it?
But the true redemption—the inner transformation—
shall be wrought by the Holy One. God is One, Holy,
Just, and Eternal. Israel is His witness.

> Thus saith the Lord, the King of Israel,
> And his Redeemer the Lord of hosts:
> I am the first, and I am the last,
> And beside Me there is no God.
> And who, as I, can proclaim—
> Let him declare it, and set it in order
>   for Me—
> Since I appointed the ancient people?
> And the things that are coming, and that
>   shall come to pass, let them declare.
> Fear ye not, neither be afraid;
> Have I not announced unto thee of old,
>   and declared it?
> And ye are My witnesses.
> Is there a God beside Me?
> Yea, there is no Rock; I know not any.[17]

But Israel's deliverance is only the first step in a universal redemption. What God desires is the salvation of
the whole world. It is Israel's unique privilege to be the
spear-point in implementing the forces of justice, compassion and holiness, thereby redeeming the world.

> For thus saith the Lord that created
>   the heavens,
> He is God;
> That formed the earth and made it,
> He established it,

[17]44:6–8.

He created it not a waste, He formed
    it to be inhabited:
I am the Lord, and there is none else.
I have not spoken in secret,
In a place of the land of darkness;
I said not unto the seed of Jacob:
"Seek ye Me in vain";
I the Lord speak righteousness,
I declare things that are right.
Assemble yourselves and come,
    draw near together,
Ye that are escaped of the nations;
They have no knowledge that carry
    the wood of their graven image,
And pray unto a god that cannot save.
Declare ye, and bring them near,
Yea, let them take counsel together:
Who hath announced this from ancient time,
And declared it of old?
Have not I the Lord?
And there is no God else beside Me;
A just God and a Saviour;
There is none beside Me.
Look unto Me, and be ye saved,
All the ends of the earth;
For I am God, and there is none else.
By Myself have I sworn,
The word is gone forth from My mouth
    in righteousness,
And shall not come back,
That unto Me every knee shall bow,
Every tongue shall swear.
Only in the Lord, shall one say of Me,
    is victory and strength;
Even to Him shall men come in confusion,
All they that were incensed against Him.

In the Lord shall all the seed of Israel
Be justified, and shall glory.[18]

MANUFACTURING AN IDOL

The idol and its maker are alike impotent. In view of
the awful majesty of the Eternal, the idol is a ridiculous
abomination. Deutero-Isaiah gives us a biting satire on
the manufacture of an idol. Of the left-overs of a log the
idolator fashions his graven image, bows down to it, wor-
ships it. "Thou art my God."

> The smith maketh an axe
> And worketh in the coals, and
>   fashioneth it with hammers,
> And worketh it with his strong arm;
> Yea, he is hungry, and his strength faileth;
> He drinketh no water, and is faint.
> The carpenter stretcheth out a line;
> He marketh it out with a pencil;
> He fitteth it with planes,
> And he marketh it out with the compasses,
> And maketh it after the figure of a man,
> According to the beauty of a man,
>   to dwell in the house.
> He heweth him down cedars,
> And taketh the ilex and the oak,
> And strengtheneth for himself
>   one among the trees of the forest;
> He planteth a bay-tree, and the rain
>   doth nourish it.
> Then a man useth it for fuel;
> And he taketh thereof, and warmeth himself;
> Yea, he kindleth it, and baketh bread;
> Yea, he maketh a god, and worshippeth it;

[18]45:18-25.

He maketh it a graven image, and falleth
   down thereto.
He burneth the half thereof in the fire;
With the half thereof he eateth flesh;
He roasteth roast, and is satisfied;
Yea, he warmeth himself, and saith:
   "Aha,
I am warm, I have seen the fire";
And the residue thereof he maketh
   a god, even his graven image;
He falleth down unto it and worshippeth,
   and prayeth unto it,
And saith: "Deliver me, for thou art my god."

They know not, neither do they understand;
For their eyes are bedaubed, that they cannot see,
And their hearts, that they cannot understand.
And none considereth in his heart,
Neither is there knowledge nor understanding
   to say:
"I have burned the half of it in the fire;
Yea, also I have baked bread upon the coals
   thereof;
I have roasted flesh and eaten it;
And shall I make the residue thereof
   an abomination?
Shall I fall down to the stock of a tree?"
He striveth after ashes,
A deceived heart hath turned him aside,
That he cannot deliver his soul, nor say:
"Is there not a lie in my right hand?"[19]

ISRAEL, THE SERVANT OF THE LORD

A lofty conception of God means a lofty view of man's
place in the world. His vision of God compels the prophet

[19] 44:12–20.

to summon his people to a profound and compelling duty. Israel is the servant of the Lord. His mission is to teach true religion to mankind. That is his inescapable destiny; for that purpose he was called into being. He shall know abuse and defeat, despondency, and despair, but his faith must never falter. His tongue must be like a sharp sword, his face "like a flint." He must carry on "till he have set truth in the earth." The tragedy is that the servant often shows himself blind and deaf to his mission. Deutero-Isaiah develops his thought in four "Servant" poems.[20]

> Behold My servant, whom I uphold;
> Mine elect, in whom My soul delighteth;
> I have put My spirit upon him,
> He shall make the right to go forth
>   to the nations.
> He shall not cry, nor lift up,
> Nor cause his voice to be heard
>   in the street.
> A bruised reed shall he not break,
> And the dimly burning wick shall
>   he not quench;
> He shall make the right to go forth
>   according to the truth.
> He shall not fail nor be crushed,
> Till he have set the right in the earth;
> And the isles shall wait for his teaching.[21]
>
> Listen, O isles, unto me,
> And hearken, ye peoples, from far:
> The Lord hath called me from the womb,
> From the bowels of my mother hath
>   He made mention of my name;

---

[20] 42:1–4; 49:1–6; 50:4–9; 52:13–53:12.   [21] 42:1–4.

And He hath made my mouth like a
  sharp sword,
In the shadow of His hand hath He hid me;
And He hath made me a polished shaft,
In His quiver hath He concealed me;
And He said unto me: "Thou art My servant,
Israel, in whom I will be glorified."
But I said: "I have laboured in vain,
I have spent my strength for nought and vanity;
Yet surely my right is with the Lord,
And my recompense with my God."
And now saith the Lord
That formed me from the womb
  to be His servant,
To bring Jacob back to Him,
And that Israel be gathered unto Him
(For I am honourable in the eyes of the Lord,
And my God is become my strength)
Yea, He saith: "It is too light a thing
  that thou shouldest be My servant
To raise up the tribes of Jacob,
And to restore the offspring of Israel;
I will also give thee for a light
  of the nations,
That My salvation may be unto the end
  of the earth."[22]

The Lord God hath given me
The tongue of them that are taught,
That I should know how to sustain
  with words him that is weary;
He wakeneth morning by morning,
He wakeneth mine ear
To hear as they that are taught.
The Lord God hath opened mine ear,

[22] 49:1–6.

And I was not rebellious,
Neither turned away backward.
I gave my back to the smiters,
And my cheeks to them that plucked off
        the hair;
I hid not my face from shame and spitting.
For the Lord God will help me;
Therefore I have not been confounded;
Therefore have I set my face like a flint,
And I know that I shall not be ashamed.
He is near that justifieth me;
Who will contend with me? let us
        stand up together;
Who is mine adversary? let him come near to me.

Behold, the Lord God will help me;
Who is he that shall condemn me?
Behold, they all shall wax old as a garment,
The moth shall eat them up.[23]

Despised and rejected of men, "a man of sorrows and acquainted with grief," the Servant knows intense suffering. The iniquity of the world rests upon him. Why? Why must Zion "receive of the Lord's hand double for all her sins"? Is it because the Servant of the Lord is the most sinful of men? Obviously this is not true, for the Servant is endowed with nobler vision, loftier purpose and finer dignity than are most men; surely Israel is more righteous than the howling Assyrians or marauding Babylonians.

Some of the Servant's chastisements were due to Israel's own shortcomings. Deutero-Isaiah, like all the prophets, did not exonerate his people of their follies. Some of his sufferings were due to the cruelties of the world, some

[23]50:4–9.

to the Servant's own nature. The sins of humanity rested
upon him because he was more sensitive than most men:

> Surely he hath borne our griefs,
> And carried our sorrows:
> Yet we did esteem him stricken,
> Smitten of God and afflicted.[24]

It is because he was the prophet of the God of justice,
loving-kindness and holiness that he felt most acutely the
bitter sting of the world's follies.

But if the Servant's spiritual endowment brought suffering it also brought the guarantee of recovery and
ultimate victory. "Because he poured out his soul unto
death," and remained true to himself and his God,

> He shall see his seed, he shall prolong his days
> And the pleasure of the Lord shall prosper in his hand.[25]

Israel, apparently slain and buried, will rise again and
triumphantly carry forward his burden as the messenger
of the Lord.[26]

DEUTERO-ISAIAH AS PROPHET

As prophet, Deutero-Isaiah differs strikingly from his
colleagues we have been considering. Unlike the other
prophets, his major concern is with prediction and comfort rather than with judgment. He does not chastise the
people for their sins as does Amos or Isaiah, Jeremiah or
Ezekiel. He summons his people to faith, not to repentance; he is anxious to bring comfort and confidence in the
future, not a realization of their wickedness and inevitable
punishment. It is the fall of Babylon, not the fall of

[24]53:4.   [25]53:10.   [26]50:13; 53:12.

Jerusalem, that he is predicting. The reason for that lay in the times in which he lived. Like the rest of the prophets, he sought to interpret the will of God in history. They lived at times when they saw the wrath of God about to explode; he lived after the explosion had taken place. Like Ezekiel after Jerusalem had fallen, he found chastisement futile and cruel. The time for comfort had come, the time for renewal of faith and hope. Hence the burden of his prophecy is divine comfort to the heavy-laden and proclamation of "good tidings to the humble." To the people of Israel who have been dragging their weary way from one exile to another, from one moral wilderness to another, the songs and prophecies of Deutero-Isaiah have been wells of living waters, converting the valley of weeping into a place of springs.

XIII

LIBERATION, FAILURE, NEW VISIONS

Not by might, nor by power, but by My spirit, saith the Lord of hosts.

ZECHARIAH 4:6.

DECREE OF CYRUS

IN THE year 539 B.C. Cyrus took possession of Babylon. All southwestern Asia, southern Mesopotamia, Syria, and Palestine came under his control. The prediction of the prophets was fulfilled; mighty Babylon was humbled. Deep in the pit of the nether world, Nebuchadrezzar was jeered by the ghosts:

> Is this the man that made the earth to tremble,
> That did shake kingdoms;
> That made the world a wilderness,
> And destroyed the cities thereof . . . ?[1]

In 538 B.C. Cyrus issued an edict liberating the Jewish colony in Babylon.[2] As many as wished might return to their native land and rehabilitate their shrine. Generous provisions were made for their journey and for the task of reconstruction. That was in keeping with his policy toward the conquered peoples that came under his rule.

[1]Isa. 14:16 (14:16–17).
[2]Ezra 1:1–4; see also 3:2–7; 5:13–16; 6:1–5.

It was an enlightened policy. It enabled him to win a large measure of loyalty from these peoples and, in the case of the Jews, helped him build a buffer province against Egypt.

A considerable number of Jews returned to their ancestral home. The records in Ezra-Nehemiah are confused and quite exaggerated. No doubt a great many more remained in the generous lap of the Tigris-Euphrates valley than returned to the stony hills of Judah. Jerusalem was a provincial, poor, and desolate city; Babylon was a cosmopolitan, thriving, exciting empire. The Jews prospered in agriculture and in commerce. Within one generation they were able to send large sums of money to Jerusalem. For once the advice given by Jeremiah was heeded. The exiles built houses, planted fields, married off their sons and daughters, and identified themselves with their new country. Why return to Jerusalem? Of the generation that had wept by the streams of Babylon, only a few aged survivors were left. The young and vigorous, reared in the shadows of the temples of Babylon, lacked the pious sentiment to surrender their comfortable homes for the ruins of Jerusalem. They were quite willing to assuage whatever irking of conscience they knew by sending some money to the city of their fathers and to remain where they were.

But a considerable number of sturdy, pious Jews did return. The first migration took place in 537 B.C. Their leaders were Zerub-babel, a descendant of the Davidic family; Joshua, a priest; and Shesh-bazzar, who served as custodian of the sacred vessels. Reverently these pioneers carried back to the Holy City the sacred vessels Nebuchadrezzar had carried off half a century earlier. Cyrus aided them with grants of money and political assistance. They found Jerusalem a desolation. Judah was overrun by squatters—Edomites, Moabites, Ammonites, Philistines, and the troublesome Samaritans. The Judean natives were a poor lot. They were the descendants of the sick, the maimed, the useless that were not worth transporting to Babylon in 586 B.C. And they intermarried with the peoples about them to a point where their Hebraic identity was difficult to ascertain.

To Jerusalem thus came the pious and courageous expedition under Zerubbabel. An ancient altar was recovered from the debris and the work of rebuilding the Temple started. In 536 B.C. the foundations of the new Temple were laid. But the initial enthusiasm soon spent itself. Difficulties presented themselves, arresting progress. One of the major troubles came from "the adversaries of Judah and Benjamin," the mixed population the exiles found in Judah who insisted on participating in the building of the Temple. Pious Israel refused them the privilege. These hybrid people would defile the sanctuary with their abominations. The Temple must be rebuilt and rebuilt in all its sanctity. Zerubbabel was adamant. "Ye have nothing to do with us in building a house unto our God; but we ourselves together will build unto the Lord, the God of Israel, as king Cyrus the king of Persia hath commanded us."[3] Bitter hatred and much strife followed. The gulf between the settled mixed population and the returned exiles grew wider. Intrigue and violence on the part of the spurned population halted the work of reconstruction for some sixteen years. Famine came upon the

[3]Ezra 4:3.

land and further discouraged the rearing of the sanctuary and the upbuilding of ruined Jerusalem.

Meanwhile a series of revolutions shook Persia. The new world-empire was tottering. Pretenders to the throne arose upon the death of Cyrus in 529 B.C.; province after province rebelled. Babylon revolted twice. Darius Hystaspes usurped the throne of Cyrus by assassinating a rival and entered upon a far-flung campaign to re-establish the sovereignty of Persia. "By the grace of Ahura-Mazda" he re-established the supremacy of his throne.

Again world-events roused the imagination of the prophets. Ezekiel had predicted the collapse of the nations before final deliverance would come to Israel. That was precisely what was happening. The world was in turmoil; Persia was reeling. Final deliverance was on the wing. But the Temple of the Lord was not yet built. Men were building comfortable homes for themselves but allowed the house of God to remain in ruins. That was an appalling sin. Judah must be roused to her sacred responsibility.

This was the inspiration of two men, Haggai and Zechariah, who sought to quicken the imagination and rouse the energies of the people.

HAGGAI AND ZECHARIAH

Both men raised their voices in the year 520 B.C. Haggai spoke several months before Zechariah. His utterances are embodied in the two short chapters that have come down to us as the book of Haggai. They are fragmentary reports of his attempt to rouse Judah to action in behalf of God and His Temple. They did build homes for themselves, he remonstrated with them; but they neglected their duties by the house of their God. For that famine came upon the land:

> Consider your ways.
> Ye have sown much, and brought in little,
> Ye eat, but ye have not enough,
> Ye drink, but ye are not filled with drink,
> Ye clothe you, but there is none warm;
> And he that earneth wages earneth wages
> For a bag with holes.[4]

That was punishment from the hands of the Almighty. In several utterances, fragmentary reports of which have come down to us, Haggai seeks to hold his people true to their duty. Once the Temple was rebuilt and its services resumed, the Messiah would come into his own. Haggai saw in Zerubbabel the anointed of the Lord.

Zechariah raised his voice in behalf of the same cause, developing his thought in a series of striking visions. He preached for some two years. Jerusalem shall arise rebuilt and reconsecrated. Let the exiles return and resume the holy task; let Zerubbabel press on with renewed vigor, for he is the Messiah:

> Ho, Zion, escape, thou that dwellest with the daughter of Babylon. . . . Sing and rejoice, O daughter of Zion; for, lo, I come, and I will dwell in the midst of thee, saith the Lord.[5]

The nations that have harassed Judah shall be overthrown; the horns of the mighty shall drop to the ground, for the will of God shall be fulfilled and His will is not realized by force. Here we have that great utterance

[4] 1:6.   [5] Zech. 2:11, 14 (2:7, 10).

which lifts Zechariah into the higher reaches of Hebrew prophecy:

Not by might, nor by power, but by My spirit, saith the Lord of hosts.[6]

A cleansing judgment shall come upon Judah; wicked-ness, like a witch, shall be banished from the land. Out of the heavens, between the peaks of two mountains of brass, come four chariots, each drawn by horses of different color—red, black, white and "grizzled bay horses." These are the avenging powers of heaven, come to purge the earth of its evils and prepare the ground for the Messiah. The chariot with the black chargers will bear the wrath of God to Babylon. The final deliverance is imminent. Zechariah smelted a crown for the Messiah.

To a delegation that had come to Jerusalem to decide whether or not to continue certain fasts, Zechariah urged the prophetic conviction that fasts and rites are of no value to God except as they fortify justice and truth. A brilliant future lay ahead for Israel. People from every nation shall come pouring into Jerusalem to seek the Lord. Jerusalem shall emerge as the "City of Truth," and Zion shall tower heavenward as "the holy mountain." The streets of Jerusalem shall resound with the happy laughter of children at play.[7]

Sing and rejoice, O daughter of Zion; for, lo, I come, and I will dwell in the midst of thee, saith the Lord. And many nations shall join themselves to the Lord in that day, and shall be My people, and I will dwell in the midst of thee.[8]

[6] 4:6.
[7] For analyses of the books of Haggai and Zechariah, see *ICC* or *CB*.
[8] 2:14–15a. Zech. 9–14 are not the work of the prophet Zechariah. See W. Emery Barnes, *CB*, Introduction, Part 3.

XIV

THE SECOND TEMPLE AND PROPHETIC ECHOES

My house shall be called
A house of prayer for all peoples.

ISAIAH 56:7.

THE SECOND TEMPLE

ON THE third day of Adar in the year 516 B.C., four and a half years after Haggai and Zechariah began to preach, the Second Temple was dedicated. It was an heroic accomplishment. Only rugged men with grim determination could build an altar under such circumstances. Half the community worked while the other half stood guard, armed against the enemy. At last the Temple was completed. A Psalm of praise welled up from the pious hearts:

> When the Lord brought back those that
>   returned to Zion,
> We were like unto them that dream.
> Then was our mouth filled with laughter,
> And our tongue with singing;
> Then said they among the nations:
> "The Lord hath done great things
>   with these."
> The Lord hath done great things with us;
> We are rejoiced.[1]

[1]Ps. 126:1-3.

But as the Temple was rising, the people were sinking in poverty. The barren land could not feed its inhabitants. Destitution gripped the poorer colonists; no doubt profiteering was resorted to by the unscrupulous. We hear of poor peasants selling their children for bread.

Rebuilding the Temple and rehabilitating the land were difficult problems, but there was a third problem that was even more perplexing: how to rehabilitate the people. Intermarriage had undone the community from within. Even priests had intermarried with the foreign peoples. It was not known who was a Hebrew and who was not.

In the year 457 B.C. a new personality assumed leadership of the feeble community and revitalized it with new energy. He was Ezra, priest and scribe, known in Jewish tradition as *the* Scribe. Another strong personality came to the fore. Nehemiah, cupbearer to the Persian monarch. Their work merged. It is difficult to disentangle the work of the two. These two men snatched Judah from certain doom and gave it a new lease on life.

Ezra returned to Jerusalem as the head of a caravan by authority of Artaxerxes, King of Persia. Men and means were placed at his disposal; even more important was the authority vested in him. "Whosoever will not do the law of thy God, and the law of the king, let judgment be executed upon him with all diligence, whether it be unto death, or to banishment, or to confiscation of goods, or to imprisonment."[2]

Primarily the zealous priest, Ezra reacted painfully and violently to the degraded state of the people. They

[2]Ezra 7:26.

had absorbed foreign blood; they had profaned "the holy seed." How could he reassert the statutes and the ordinances under such circumstances? God must be implored; the people must be purged. A dramatic and cruel reform was instituted by Ezra. In a solemn convention he ordered the dissolution of all mixed marriages. Homes were disrupted; families were torn asunder. A deep misery was released by a pious priest in an effort to purify the race.[3]

Nehemiah held the office of cupbearer in the Persian court. From travellers and visitors to the court he heard of the misery in Judah. He could not remain at peace in a palace in Persia. Jerusalem was calling. He surrendered his position and returned to the ruined city of his fathers. He surveyed the ruins, alone at night, and wept. With fanatic zeal he set to work. Patriots rallied round him. Against many and severe odds he cleared the ground of its accumulation of fifty years and more of debris, freed the land of its despoilers, armed its citizenry, rehabilitated the shrine and took measures to reform the economic structure of the land.

Ezra and Nehemiah were striking, powerful personalities. Their work fused in one mighty effort to lift the nation from the grave. Ezra was the Scribe and builder of Israel's faith. Stern, unyielding, relentless, cruel in his reforms, his work and Nehemiah's blended into one. They reared anew the collapsed altar, and rehabilitated the shattered nation. Ezra made the first sacred canon of the Scriptures and carried forward the work of Ezekiel in establishing the Synagogue.

[3]Ezra 9–10.

Against this background we read the last prophetic utterances.

Chapters 56–66 of the book of Isaiah, as we have seen, belong to this period. Here the prophetic voice is heard in characteristic eloquence. The wrath of God is invoked upon the despoilers of Israel, both foreign and native. Social misery is attacked; false religion is denounced; high prophetic ideals are enunciated anew; a summons to new courage and renewed faith is sounded.

It is the sins of the people that have estranged them from their God:

> Behold, the Lord's hand is not shortened,
>   that it cannot save,
> Neither His ear heavy, that it cannot hear;
> But your iniquities have separated
> Between you and your God,
> And your sins have hid His face from you,
> That He will not hear.
> For your hands are defiled with blood,
> And your fingers with iniquity;
> Your lips have spoken lies,
> Your tongue muttereth wickedness.
> None sueth in righteousness,
> And none pleadeth in truth;
> They trust in vanity, and speak lies,
> They conceive mischief, and bring forth
>   iniquity.
>
> .   .   .   .
>
> Therefore is justice far from us,
> Neither doth righteousness overtake us;
> We look for light, but behold darkness,

For brightness, but we walk in gloom.
We grope for the wall like the blind,
Yea, as they that have no eyes do we grope;
We stumble at nonday as in the twilight;
We are in dark places like the dead.
We all growl like bears,
And mourn sore like doves;
We look for right, but there is none;
For salvation, but it is far off from us.[4]

Ritual, not religion, is what the people were practising.
The classic accents of prophecy are heard denouncing
immoral religion:

Cry aloud, spare not,
Lift up thy voice like a horn,
And declare unto My people
    Their transgression,
And to the house of Jacob their sins.
Yet they seek Me daily,
And delight to know My ways;
As a nation that did righteousness,
And forsook not the ordinance of their God,
They ask of Me righteous ordinances,
They delight to draw near unto God.

"Wherefore have we fasted, and
    Thou seest not?
Wherefore have we afflicted our soul,
    and Thou takest no knowledge?"—
Behold, in the day of your fast
    ye pursue your business,
And exact all your labours.
Behold, ye fast for strife and
    contention,

[4] 59:1-4; 9-11.

And to smite with the fist
   of wickedness;
Ye fast not this day
So as to make your voice
   to be heard on high.
Is such the fast that I have chosen?
The day for a man to afflict his soul?
Is it to bow down his head as a bulrush,
And to spread sackcloth and ashes
   under him?
Wilt thou call this a fast,
And an acceptable day to the Lord?
Is not this the fast that I have chosen?
To loose the fetters of wickedness,
To undo the bands of the yoke?
Is it not to deal thy bread to the hungry,
And that thou bring the poor that are cast out
   to thy house?
When thou seest the naked, that thou cover him,
And that thou hide not thyself from thine
   own flesh?
Then shall thy light break forth
   as the morning,
And thy healing shall spring forth speedily;
And thy righteousness shall go before thee,
The glory of the Lord shall be thy rearward.
Then shalt thou call, and the Lord will answer;
Thou shalt cry, and He will say: "Here I am."[5]

In a passage of contagious enthusiasm, the unknown poet, generally called by scholars Trito-Isaiah, flings a vision of the future:

Arise, shine, for thy light is come,
And the glory of the Lord is risen
   upon thee.

[5] 58:1–9a.

For, behold, darkness shall cover the earth,
And gross darkness the peoples;
But upon thee the Lord will arise,
And His glory shall be seen upon thee.
And nations shall walk at thy light,
And kings at the brightness of thy rising.[6]

OBADIAH

The book of Obadiah is the shortest in the Bible. It consists of only twenty-one verses, and they are badly confused. The central theme, however, is clear. Edom shall be dragged from her rocky fastnesses and despoiled, for she helped rob her brother Jacob and showed no mercy. It was left to Obadiah to be consistently revengeful.

MALACHI

Like Obadiah, Malachi—or the prophet to whom this name was attached—spoke in the period of gloom while Ezra-Nehemiah were struggling with the problems of reconstruction.[7] Like Obadiah, too, he invokes vengeance upon Edom. But he goes beyond it. He seeks to revive the faith of his people. He breathes courage and enthusiasm. If distress hangs over the land, it is because the people have neglected the Temple and its sacrifices. The corrupt priests were offering the lame, the crippled, the diseased upon the altars of Him who requires the pure and the holy. "Will a man rob God? Yet ye rob Me."[8] But graver sin hung over the people.

And I will come near to you to judgment;
And I will be a swift witness

[6] 60:1–3.
[7] For analyses of Obadiah and Malachi, see *CB*.
[8] 3:8.

> Against the sorcerers, and against
> the adulterers,
> And against the false swearers;
> And against those that oppress the
> hireling in his wages,
> The widow, and the fatherless,
> And that turn aside the stranger
> from his right,
> And fear not Me,
> Saith the Lord of hosts.[9]

This was practised despite the professed belief in the same God.

> Have we not all one father?
> Hath not one God created us?
> Why do we deal treacherously every man
> against his brother,
> Profaning the covenant of our fathers?[10]

To the bragging skeptics of his day Malachi addressed himself with a reaffirmation of his faith in a just God. In His book of remembrance He has inscribed the faithful, and the day will come when the righteous will be separated from the wicked. Ultimate victory shall be with the righteous.

> But unto you that fear My name
> Shall the sun of righteousness arise
> with healing on its wings.[11]

"Malachi" was probably not the real name of the prophet. The word occurs in the Hebrew text and means "My messenger." It is eminently fitting that such an

[9] 3:5.　　　　[10] 2:10.　　　　[11] 3:20 (4:2).

appellation be given to the man whose words complete the canon of biblical prophecy.

JOEL

One more prophet whose book has come down to us bearing his name remains to be included in our procession of prophets. He is the prophet Joel.

The book of Joel is a flaming scroll of woes. Plague, drought, and famine came upon the land. Gardens and orchards, fields and forests were one charred desolation.

> The field is wasted,
> The land mourneth;
> For the corn is wasted,
> The new wine is dried up,
> The oil languisheth . . .
> The vine is withered,
> And the fig-tree languisheth;
> The pomegranate-tree, the palm-tree
>   also, and the apple-tree,
> Even all the trees of the fields are
>   withered;
> For joy is withered away from the sons
>   of men.
>
> . . . .
>
> The grains shrivel under their hoes;
> The garners are laid desolate,
> The barns are broken down;
> For the corn is withered.
> How do the beasts groan![12]

The harvests have shrivelled into dust; the beasts are perishing; "the flame hath set ablaze all the trees of the

[12]1:10, 12, 17.

field"; all the streams have dried up. Even the beasts of the field pant prayers to God for mercy.

This is a visitation from God for the sins of the people. The day of the Lord is nigh. Priests and people must repent if God is to show pity. He is gracious and merciful and will repent Him of the evil. The devouring locusts will disappear; the rains will return; the earth will revive; the spirit of the Lord will be poured out upon all flesh. The unclean aliens shall be exterminated. The Day of the Lord shall be a day of terror for the evil-doers:

> Multitudes, multitudes in the valley of decision!
> For the Day of the Lord is near in the valley of
>   decision.
> The sun and the moon have become black,
> And the stars withdraw their shining.
> And the Lord shall roar from Zion,
> And utter His voice from Jerusalem,
> And the heavens and the earth shall shake;
> But the Lord will be a refuge unto His people,
> And a stronghold to the children of Israel.[13]

We know nothing of Joel's personal history beyond his name and the name of his father. Scholars are in wide disagreement as to the date of his book. Some think it is pre-exilic and place it in the year 737 B.C., thus making Joel a contemporary of Hosea. Others would place the book between the years 640 and 609 B.C., roughly the period of Isaiah. Still others consider the book as post-exilic and ascribe it to the year 500 B.C. or later.[14]

[13]4:14–16.
[14]See S. R. Driver, *CB* to Joel, Introduction.

XV

TWO PARABLES

Thy people shall be my people and thy God my God.
RUTH 1:16.

WATERFALL AND RESERVOIR

WE HAVE stood in the presence of the masters of Hebrew prophecy. We have summoned them one by one from the long ago. We have observed their tremendous passion for God and His will in the affairs of men; we have tried to catch something of their awesome eloquence. Like lightning in the night, they flashed across their dark centuries and disappeared, bequeathing mankind with a vision of men possessed by the Divine. We have no more prophets to summon from the pages of the Old Testament. But that does not mean that prophecy died in Israel.

We might liken these prophetic figures we have been studying to mighty waterfalls. Brilliant, radiant, dazzling, they plunged from the high cliffs of inspiration to the ground of the every-day world with its sins, stupidities, and cruelties. Their teachings formed a tremendous reservoir of moral idealism in Israel. Prophecy ceased being spectacular with inspired eloquence; but, penetrating to the very life of the masses and their teachers, it nurtured the roots of personal piety and social idealism. This expressed itself in every sphere of the life of Israel.

We see the force of prophecy in the legislation of priests, scribes, and rabbis; we feel its pulse in much of the Bible narrative and rabbinic homily; we see it expressed in the didactic language of the sages. It is a potent force in the liturgy of Israel. The spectacular prophets, not prophecy, ceased in biblical Israel. Prophecy went underground and nurtured the moral life. The prophet's own hope came true: the choice spirit of Israel took root downward and bore fruit upward. For the next chapter in the history of Hebrew prophecy, we must turn to the Wisdom literature of Israel and to Israel's legislation, biblical and rabbinic.

RUTH AND JONAH

In two parables, especially, the spirit of Hebrew prophecy speaks in vigorous accents. The two are the books of Ruth and Jonah.

Both issue from the moral miseries that attended the Ezra reformation; both are protests against the spirit of racialism that gripped Israel; both are pleas for the universal.

The lovely book of Ruth tells in tender words the story of a non-Jewish young woman—Ruth of the land of Moab —who became a Jewess so completely and so nobly that it was from her body and her spirit that eventually came King David, Israel's greatest king and psalmist. The Messiah himself, when he comes, according to Jewish tradition, will be a scion of the Davidic family; hence, he will carry in his veins and in his soul something of the Moabitish Ruth. Rabbinic masters made her the heroine of the festival of Shabuoth for the reason that Ruth,

like Israel at the foot of Sinai, embraced the discipline
issuing from the revelation of God.

Ruth's acceptance of the people Israel and the God
of Israel was complete. Her pledge of loyalty is among
the choice pronouncements in Hebrew lore:

Entreat me not to leave thee, and to return from
following after thee; for whither thou goest, I will go;
and where thou lodgest, I will lodge; thy people shall be
my people; and thy God my God; where thou diest, will
I die, and there will I be buried; the Lord do so to me,
and more also, if aught but death part thee and me.[1]

Could a more religious answer be given to the racialism
of Ezra that required Jewish men to divorce their non-
Jewish wives and that would not grant the Samaritans
the opportunity to co-operate in building the Temple
dedicated to the Lord of the Universe and the Father of
all men? An Amos or an Isaiah would not have spoken
in the manner of the unknown author of the book of Ruth,
but the word and the spirit are the same.

Jonah, a Hebrew prophet, is commissioned by God to
carry His word to wicked Nineveh so that that heathen
city may have the opportunity to save itself by means
of repentance. Jonah, a savage fanatic, a prophet in
whom religion is dead, dislikes the commission. He boards
a ship sailing in the opposite direction from Nineveh,
thus seeking to run away from the universal God he pro-
fesses. A storm overtakes the ship; the heathen sailors see
in it a warning from God for some one's sin. Who was
the evil-doer who has brought this wrath of God upon
the ship? Lots are cast and Jonah is identified as the

[1] 1:16-17.

guilty one. A satiric scene is presented; the heathen sailors are praying to their gods while the Hebrew prophet is asleep. Aroused and told of what happened, Jonah does the only decent thing that is reported of him in the story; he suggests that he be thrown overboard so that the sea may be calmed and the ship and crew saved. The heathen sailors are reluctant to deal so lightly with a human life; they offer their prayers and finally do throw him into the sea.

But that is not the end of Jonah. He still has his lesson to learn and his commission to perform. "The Lord prepared a great fish to swallow up Jonah; and Jonah was in the belly of the fish three days and three nights." That gives Jonah the opportunity to reflect upon his conduct and to offer his prayers. Then the fish vomits out Jonah upon the dry land.

Again the call comes to him to go to Nineveh and speak the word of God. This time Jonah obeys. Walking through the streets of that great city, he proclaims: "Yet forty days and Nineveh shall be destroyed." Another miracle, as great as the fish incident, occurs. The people of Nineveh, hearing the warning spoken by this foreign prophet, repent. King and pauper alike put on sackcloth and sit in ashes. A fast is proclaimed. Even the animals repent. Thus the city is saved.

The only unhappy man is Jonah. To the merciful God of heaven and earth he prays: "O Lord, was not this my saying, when I was yet in mine own country? Therefore I fled beforehand unto Tarshish; for I knew that Thou art a gracious God, and compassionate, long-suffering, and abundant in mercy, and repentest Thee of the evil.

Therefore now, O Lord, take, I beseech Thee, my life from me; for it is better for me to die than to live."[2] Jonah has not learned his lesson yet.

Hoping against hope that the city will be destroyed, the prophet takes a position outside the city from which he may observe whatever may happen. Miraculously a gourd springs up and shields the unhappy prophet from the heat of the day. But a worm soon kills the plant, and Jonah is left exposed to the merciless heat. Jonah again prays for death. The voice of God then penetrates to his narrow heart: "Art thou greatly angry for the gourd? . . . Should not I have pity on Nineveh, on that great city, wherein are more than sixscore thousand persons and cannot discern between their right hand and their left hand, and also much cattle?"[3]

The book is clearly an attack on the narrow, tribal Judaism of the day, and a plea for universality. God is one and mankind is one. In Nineveh or Jerusalem, on land or at the bottom of the sea, God is, and His will prevails. Pious Israelites or heathen Ninevites are alike His children. His desire is that they repent of their evils, save themselves, and live. The rabbinic masters carried this prophetic spirit into Judaism and made it part of the liturgy of the Synagogue. They made the book of Jonah part of the liturgy for the Day of Atonement.

Obviously, to read the book of Jonah as history is to become involved in a mesh of highly embarrassing miracles and to pervert a great prophetic message into ludicrous nonsense. The book is Hebrew prophecy at its highest level, told in the form of a parable. Montefiore rightly

[2] 4:2-3.   [3] 4:9, 11.

characterizes the book of Jonah as "the triumph of Judaism." "The author of Jonah," this scholar writes, "takes rank with the Second Isaiah as a master-builder of Judaism. The one teaches the doctrine of absolute monotheism, the other the doctrine of human brotherhood to which the divine unity leads us on. The one lays down the nature of Israel's mission, the other illustrates it. Service and not privilege, or rather, the privilege of service; that is the reason of Israel's separateness and that is its justification."[4]

[4]*The Bible for Home Reading*, Part II, pp. 419–420.

XVI

CONCLUSION

. . . make you a new heart and a new spirit.
                            EZEKIEL 18:31.

TWO MISCONCEPTIONS

THE reader who has followed the present writer thus far
in the volume must be aware of two common misconcep-
tions that prevail regarding the Hebrew prophets. Both
issue from a basic misunderstanding of the nature of
Hebrew prophecy.

THE PROPHETS AND THE REFORMERS

One misunderstanding is the frequent association of
the Hebrew prophets with one school or another of economic reform or political theory. The Hebrew prophets
knew nothing of socialism, syndicalism, anarchism or any
other economic or political "ism." They were, of course,
impassioned champions of social justice; they attacked
vehemently and bitterly the malefactors of wealth, the
abusers of power, the greedy and the unscrupulous of
their times. But they did so not by way of advancing one
economic formula or another; they had no economic
formulæ of any kind. If we find a political system implied in their preachments, it is a theocracy. One force
and one force only gave direction to their thinking and

eloquence to their utterances, making them impassioned protagonists of justice, mercy, and holiness in the lives of men and communities. That one force was the will of God.

They did not speculate as to the nature of the will of God. They knew what they meant by it. So real and overwhelming was the will of God to them that they did not so much as suspect that it might be a blank term to others. "The peculiarity of the prophets was that they never aimed at depicting or defining the divine nature. They wished only to show, just as their souls experienced it, what God means to man, and what man should be before God."[1] The social implications of the will of God they expressed in ringing words. Micah has summarized their thought once and forever in his great formula: "It hath been told thee, O man, what is good and what the Lord doth require of thee: only to do justly, to love mercy, and to walk humbly with thy God."[2] Unlike Plato, they did not delve into the nature of justice.

The point to note is that the prophets did not seek to bring justice into the world by merely reorganizing the external forms of society. They sought a transformation of the inner man. A nobler man in a more just world, a new heart and a new mind, mankind speaking a purer tongue—these would come if the will of God prevailed in the lives of men and nations.

THE PROPHETS AND JESUS

The second common misconception of the prophets is crediting them with the foretelling of far-off events, cen-

[1] Leo Baeck, *The Essence of Judaism* (N. Y., 1936), p. 90.
[2] Micah 6:8.

turies removed, on the basis of some occult power of prediction. We have discussed this in the opening chapter of the present work. We note here the application of this misunderstanding to the announcement of the coming of Christ.

Isaiah, especially, is credited with the foretelling of the coming of Jesus. The solid fact is that there are some seven hundred years between Isaiah and Jesus. Isaiah may have hoped for a type of leader to arise which, later, Jesus approximated; but that is not to say that Isaiah announced his coming. This supposed prediction rests on a misunderstanding of the verses in Isaiah that are involved, and on a more basic misunderstanding of the nature of Hebrew prophecy.[3]

There is much speculation as to the future in Christian thought and Jewish Kabbalistic vagaries in the writings of the prophets. The assertion is advanced as religious dogma that the second coming of Jesus is definitely predicted. The collapse of the world is predicted on the basis of other verses. During the Italian-Ethiopian war of 1936, Ezekiel was quoted as having predicted the conquest of Ethiopia.[4] This is unworthy use of prophetic literature.

STRENGTH AND WEAKNESS OF THE PROPHETS

The strength and the weakness of the prophets lie in the fact that they did not implement their ideals. They left them in the rarefied air of inspired speech. Amos attacked the corruption of his day, but he did not advance

[3]See G. B. Gray, *ICC* to Isaiah 7:14–16. J. Skinner, *CB* to same passage.
[4]*N. Y. Times*, Letter to the Editor, May 17, 1936.

a method of righting it nor of preventing its recurrence. In the face of invasion Isaiah urged faith upon the distracted King Ahaz; that was sublime faith for a prophet, but the king was hard-pressed by the enemy's sword and needed a practical, immediate method of deliverance. Isaiah had none to offer him. Jeremiah could attack—and, as history shows, rightly so—the alliances with Egypt in the face of Babylonian invasion, but what practical solution did he have to offer to King Zedekiah? The prophets were carried by lofty visions of a new heaven and a new earth, but they had no programs to help men realize these ideals. The only one who did advance a definite program is Ezekiel.

While this is a weakness, it is also a source of strength. The techniques and the formulæ change with the times. New circumstances call for different approaches to the problems of mankind. Programs, therefore, are comparatively short-lived. The visions of justice, mercy, holiness are eternal. The prophets allied themselves with the eternal. They were satisfied to give direction to the aspirations of their fellows and to let others find the ways of their realization. The geniuses in the realm of religion, it has been said, "are the lightning rods which are first struck by the fire of God. Their minds are sensitized to receive the impressions of divine justice, love, and holiness."[5] The prophets made their profound contribution to the moral life of mankind by serving as lightning rods, bringing the fire of God down to earth.

[5]Samuel S. Cohon, *What We Jews Believe* (Cincinnati, 1931), p. 131.

BOOKS SUGGESTED FOR
FURTHER STUDY

HISTORY

Jastrow, Morris, *Hebrew and Babylonian Traditions*, N. Y., Scribners, 1914. Important for an understanding of Babylonian backgrounds to Bible traditions.

Kittel, Rudolf, *Great Men and Movements in Israel*, N. Y., Macmillan, 1929. Scholarly presentations of the men who shaped Hebrew destiny, from Moses to the Maccabees.

Lods, Adolphe, *Israel: From Its Beginnings to the Middle of the Eighth Century*, N. Y., Knopf, 1932. Excellent for the pre-Israelite history of Canaan; thoroughly scholarly, popular in style. In the *History of Civilization* Series.

Olmstead, A. T., *History of Palestine and Syria*, N. Y., Scribners, 1931. Accurate, thoroughly reliable.

Price, Ira Maurice, *The Dramatic Story of the Old Testament*, N. Y., Revell, 1929. Vividly written, reliable, it is one of the best one-volume histories of the Bible period. It is well integrated with the Bible text and fully illustrated.

Smith, George Adam, *The Historical Geography of the Holy Land*, London, Hodder and Stoughton, 1906. Vivid, scholarly; a fine combination of the scholarly and the poetic.

Smith, Henry Preserved, *Old Testament History*, N. Y., Scribners, 1923. A standard work; the most comprehensive one-volume history of the Old Testament.

BIBLE

Baldwin, E. C., *Types of Literature in the Old Testament*, N. Y., Nelson, 1929. A good introduction to the literary study of the Old Testament.

Bewer, J. A., *Literature of the Old Testament*, N. Y., Columbia Press, 1933. Fine insight into the literary values of the Old Testament, historically considered.

Driver, S. R., *An Introduction to the Literature of the Old Testament*, N. Y., Scribners, 1923. A standard work by a master in Bible scholarship.

Goodspeed, Edgar J., *The Story of the Old Testament*, Chicago, University of Chicago Press, 1934. An excellent primer in Bible study.

Montefiore, Claude G., *The Bible for Home Reading*, Macmillan, 1902. The results of Bible scholarship are utilized; good for the layman, though meant for young readers; scientific and religious in spirit.

PROPHETS

Buttenwieser, Moses, *The Prophets of Israel*, N. Y., Macmillan, 1914. Stimulating and radical in its treatment of Bible text.

Cornill, Carl H., *The Prophets of Israel*, Chicago, Open Court, 1901. Well written, sympathetic biographies, for the layman.

Driver, S. R., *The Book of the Prophet Jeremiah*, N. Y., Scribners, 1906. The text of the book Jeremiah edited in the light of Bible science; special attention given to the chronologic order of the book.

Lods, Adolphe, *The Prophets and the Rise of Judaism,* London, Paul, Trench, Trubner & Co., 1937. A basic analysis of the development of Hebrew prophecy, clearly written; a continuation of the author's *Israel.*

Loehr, Max, *A History of Religion in the Old Testament,* N. Y., Scribners, 1936. A brief and systematic presentation; good for a beginner.

Montefiore, Claude G., *Hibbert Lectures,* London, Williams and Norgate, 1897. Stimulating, scientific and religious in spirit; still valid in its factual basis.

Skinner, John, *Prophecy and Religion,* London, Cambridge University Press, 1922. A basic study by a recognized master.

Smith, George Adam, *The Book of Isaiah,* N. Y., Doran, 1905. *The Book of the Twelve Prophets,* N. Y., A. C. Armstrong & Son, 1905. Stimulating, critical and reverent studies by a recognized master.

Smith, J. M. Powis, *The Prophets and Their Times,* Chicago, University of Chicago Press, 1925. Especially good for the integration of the prophets with the historic backgrounds; by a highly regarded scholar.

Margolis, Max L., *Micah,* Phila., Jewish Publication Society, 1908. A conservative treatment of the text, from the Jewish point of view.

The prophetic books in the *Cambridge Bible for Schools and Colleges,* London, Cambridge University Press; N. Y., Macmillan, and in the *International Critical Commentary,* Edinburgh, T. & T. Clark; N. Y.,

Scribners. The first is the more conservative and readable; the latter is exhaustive and radical. The latter, especially, is for the advanced student.

SUPPLEMENTARY BIBLIOGRAPHY

Albright, W. F., *From Stone Age to Christianity*, Baltimore, Johns Hopkins Press, 1940; Anchor Book

Anderson, Bernhard W., *Understanding the Old Testament*, Englewood, N. J., Prentice-Hall, 1957

Blank, Sheldon, *Prophetic Faith in Isaiah*, N. Y., Harper & Bros., 1958

Interpreter's Bible, to the prophetic books, N. Y., and Nashville, Abingdon Press

Orlinsky, Harry M., *Ancient Israel*, Ithaca, Cornel University Press, 1954

Rowley, H. H. ed., *The Old Testament and Modern Study*, Oxford, 1951

REFERENCES

J. Hastings, *A Dictionary of the Bible* in 5 volumes;

J. Hastings, *Dictionary of the Bible* in one volume;

J. Hastings, *Encyclopædia of Religion and Ethics*. Indispensable for the student of religion. Edinburgh, T. & T. Clark; N. Y., Scribners.

A. S. Peakes, *Commentary on the Bible* in one volume. London and N. Y., Nelson.

INDEX

INDEX

Ahab, 3, 40
Ahaz, 58, 59
Ahikam, 125
Amaziah, 24, 25, 26
Ammon, 30
Amon, 86
Amos, 5, 7, 20, 23–37, 42, 46, 49, 53, 62, 67
Anathoth, 108
Arabia, 83
Ascension of Isaiah, 66
Ashdod, 56, 60, 69
Asherah, 16, 19, 21
Ashtar-Chemosh, 20
Ashtoreth, 19
Ashurbanipal, 82
Assyria, 55, 58 ff., 66, 67, 68, 82 ff.
Astarte, 19

Baal, 16 ff.
Babylon, 82 ff.
Baeck, L., 222
Bailey and Kent, 57
Barnes, W. E., 204
Baruch, 125 ff.
Beth-el, 23 ff., 42
Buttenwieser, M., 14

Carchemish, 104, 122, 126
Characteristics of the prophets, 1–8
Chemosh, 16, 21
Cheney, 38, 78
Cohon, S. S., 224
Cooke, G. A., 158, 172
Cornill, C. H., 49
Cyrus, 175 ff.

Damascus, 30, 59
Darius Hystaspes, 202
David, 3, 12, 75
Davidson, A. B., 107, 158
Day of the Lord, 34, 73, 94, 214
Deutero-Isaiah, 175–198
Deuteronomy, 15 ff., 86 ff., 115–117
Driver, S. R., 15, 27, 58, 87, 92, 107

Ebed-melech, 134

Edom, 30, 59, 83
Egypt, 68, 82 ff.
Elam, 83
Elephantine, 145
Elijah, 4, 15
Elisha, 9, 13
Elkosh, 96
Emmanuel sign, 57
Esarhaddon, 82, 84
Ezekiel, 7, 14, 130, 138, 151–174
Ezra, 206 ff.

Freedom of will, 166 ff.

Gaza, 59
Gedaliah, 138
Gehenna, 121
Genesis Rabbah, 50
Gray, G. B., 58, 223

Habakkuk, 98 ff., 147
Haggai, 202 ff.
Haurai, 83
Hezekiah, 59, 61, 82
Hilkiah, 16
Hinnom, 16, 22, 121
Hosea, 7, 20, 36, 38–50, 62, 65, 67, 159, 164

Idolatry, 15–22
Isaiah, 2, 7, 14, 31, 51–76, 79, 159, 164
Ishtar, 19

Jahu, 145
Jehoahaz, 93
Jehoiakim, 93, 106, 126
Jehoshaphat, 11
Jephthah, 22
Jereboam II, 24, 42, 57
Jeremiah, 2, 4, 7, 14, 22, 102–143, 159, 166
Jerome, Saint, 98
Jerusalem, 16, 55, 62, 63, 65, 69, 75, 94, 137, 144 ff.
Jesus, 222 ff.
Jezebel, 4

231